THE PARADISE NOTEBOOKS

The Paradise Notebooks

90 MILES ACROSS THE SIERRA NEVADA

Richard J. Nevle
Steven Nightingale

Illustrations by Mattias Lanas

COMSTOCK PUBLISHING ASSOCIATES
an imprint of
CORNELL UNIVERSITY PRESS
Ithaca and London

First published 2022 by Cornell University Press

Printed in the United States of America

Library of Congress Cataloging-in-Publication Data

Names: Nevle, Richard J., author. | Nightingale, Steven, author.
Title: The paradise notebooks : 90 miles across the Sierra Nevada / Richard J. Nevle & Steven Nightingale.
Description: Ithaca [New York] : Cornell University Press, 2022. | Includes bibliographical references.
Identifiers: LCCN 2021030359 (print) | LCCN 2021030360 (ebook) | ISBN 9781501762697 (hardcover) | ISBN 9781501762802 (pdf) | ISBN 9781501762819 (epub)
Subjects: LCSH: Natural history—Sierra Nevada (Calif. and Nev.) | Sierra Nevada (Calif. and Nev.) | LCGFT: Essays.
Classification: LCC QH104.5.S54 N48 2022 (print) | LCC QH104.5.S54 (ebook) | DDC 508.794/4—dc23
LC record available at https://lccn.loc.gov/2021030359
LC ebook record available at https://lccn.loc.gov/2021030360

To

Lucy Blake and to Gabriella Nightingale, *las viajeras deslumbrantes*

—SN

For

Nancy, Deborah, and Sophie, my teachers

—RJN

Inebriate of air—am I—
And Debauchee of Dew—
Reeling—thro' endless summer days—
From inns of molten Blue—

—Emily Dickinson

If one has the humility to call upon one's instinct, upon the elemental, there is in sensuousness a kind of cosmic joy.

—Jean Giono

Heaven makes things easy. So do not make them difficult.

—Ibn Abbad of Ronda

CONTENTS

PREFACE

I was five the first time I saw them, only a faint glow in the distance. Heading to the Big Bend, traveling west, I'd woken at dawn in the back seat of my family's Rambler station wagon. My parents had driven the night, leaving just after sunset to avoid the searing heat of August—and the internecine warfare that would have otherwise ensued in the cramped back seat. My brothers and I had fallen asleep somewhere on the outskirts of Houston, our station wagon trundling west on I-10 out into the starry darkness.

I awoke to the rainy scent of creosote—and a swell of violet earth curving like a wing across the horizon. "Those are mountains, son, the Del Nortes," my father told me, sipping coffee from a thermos.

"Mountains?" I asked.

I fell silent. I stared hard at the great rise of rock, which pulled me with an ineluctable gravity.

I am still drawn to mountains, just as I was then, by feral curiosity and aesthetic impulse. Many claim to have found God in the mountains. I don't know what God is, but I admit to having sought her there too.

Whatever my search, I have found that the pursuit of scientific inquiry—its own, necessarily limited kind of truth-seeking—can be as much an act of devotion as it is scholarly meditation. For to pay attention to the world, to seek its stories, to run your fingers along some crack of rock or furrow of tree bark, to admire a raptor in flight, to look, closely, at the construction of a previously unencountered wildflower—to wonder and to seek answers to how these things might have come to be in the world—are themselves acts of devotion, ways of knowing, ways of longing for communion. As Diane Ackerman has written, "There is a way of beholding nature that is itself a form of prayer."

I saw the Sierra Nevada for the first time when I was twenty-three, again driving west, this time with the woman who would become my wife and the mother of our child. Yet I recognized the place, for years earlier the cool air, the sparkling Sierra granite, the deep green of conifer forests had visited me in a dream—a dream of a place I would come upon after dying.

We were on our way to California so that I could begin my doctoral studies in geology. In the years to follow I would spend two summers of my graduate career living in mountains in the remote Arctic wilderness of East Greenland, much of it alone, mapping networks of mineral-filled veins—ancient passages of water through stone.

Stone, I found, does not reveal its secrets readily. I spent many seasons working in windowless labs, slicing and crushing and grinding the rock samples I'd sledge-hammered from outcrops so I could relentlessly scrutinize them with a battery of fragile, complicated, and expensive instruments. All in order to squeeze a story out of them only faintly limned during my field work in Greenland. Slowly the pieces were assembling themselves, though I didn't know it at the time. I would discover hidden in the rocks a story of how climate had changed in the ancient Arctic over tens of millions of years, as Greenland heaved upward and tore from Scandinavia, and then as a warm tongue of the North Atlantic probed the widening gulf between the landmasses.

Like plate tectonics, science works in slow motion; and thick ignorance, I would learn, is a landscape we must wander through en route to discovery. Yet still I was plagued by doubt, not so much of a scientific nature but rather that which emerged from a gnawing uncertainty about the value of my focused intellectual effort in a world so plagued by human suffering and environmental destruction—the latter of which I was becoming increasingly aware. What was I doing for the world?

It wasn't until I was a few years on in my graduate work that I returned to the Sierra. I couldn't believe it had taken me so long. Like so many others before me, I found a kind of homecoming—a place where I could breathe deeply, where I could listen to the world in a way I seldom could otherwise in the harried, anxiety-ridden life I lived as a graduate student. I slowed to listen to the sounds of streams tumbling over stones and wind hushing in conifer boughs, and to immerse my body in cold mountain streams. In the Sierra, I found a rare and beatific peace.

In the two decades since my daughter's birth, I have hiked and backpacked with my family every year in the Sierra backcountry. We have wandered up trails into the range's east and west flanks, spending days swimming in frigid lakes, wandering across ridgetops, getting lost, finding ourselves again, falling asleep beneath star-dusted skies. We have walked high mountain meadows beneath the moon, listening to the eerie songs of coyotes and singing back to them and they to us. We've come upon wild black bears lumbering through the forest, lifting massive, rotting tree trunks, spinning them like toys, shredding them to bits as they excavated for insects. A ranger, who would later become a dear friend, once led me to a high saddle near the range's crest in the Yosemite high country. Through her binoculars, she spotted a prairie falcon still several miles distant. Within minutes, the bird was upon us, soaring only meters above. Its speckled body and sharp wings sliced across the sky. A second later the falcon was gone, hurtling off toward the jagged horizon, leaving me stunned that such a wholly perfect thing could exist. With other companions I have sought out rare butterflies and endangered frogs endemic to the Sierra—if for no other reason than to bear witness to their existence. There is something numinous and joyful in these encounters, a way in which the boundary between the world we sense and the world that is beyond our senses becomes, for the briefest of moments, thin—almost transparent.

~ ~ ~

A few years ago, California endured its most severe drought in a millennium, resulting in the deaths of hundreds of millions of trees in the Sierra Nevada's forested western flank. This, of course, is only one of the myriad devastations occurring across our planet exacerbated by human-caused warming. The black parade of wreckage grows in scope and magnitude and severity daily. To live at this time in history, if we are half-conscious, is to live at a time in which one wakes each day to a world grieving for what has been lost, for what is being lost, for what will be lost. In dreams I see the Greenland glaciers that I walked across as a younger man, their water trickling from rotting ice into the ocean. I wake to read of the disappearance of summer sea ice, on which I'd seen hundreds of seals basking, their cacophonous barking audible on days I'd mapped near the coast. In the Sierra, I've journeyed up into the mountains to see grizzled bodies of ice, which in the decades since I'd moved to California ended their active lives as glaciers. I've looked out across undulating ribs of mountains onto miles of dead conifer forest, the trees' needles as brown and as brittle as rust.

Terry Tempest Williams wrote that it is time "to step out from behind our personas—whatever they might be: educators, activists, biologists, geologists, writers, farmers, ranchers, and bureaucrats—and admit we are lovers, engaged in an erotics of place. Loving the land. Honoring its mysteries. Acknowledging, embracing the spirit of place, there is nothing more legitimate and there is nothing more true."

In August of 2017, my friend Steven Nightingale and I backpacked ninety miles across the Sierra Nevada with our families. As we walked, we talked about the way our work—mine in environmental science, Steven's in poetry and fiction—had a common thread, because of our inclination to venture outside our specialties. We talked of the way that the qualities of the Sierra held such power and wonder, of how they might be honored and understood by using the whole mind—that is, by bringing to this legendary mountain range the insights, taken together, of science, of natural history, of poetry, storytelling, and spirituality. We thought such an approach could offer to readers a new and newly respectful pathway of understanding the natural splendors of the Sierra Nevada—and by extension, something larger.

In this book, we want the reader to walk with us and discover a vision of the land that, not being confined within one way of study, is more complete and integrated. Our intention is that the reader might arrive with us at the moment when the different perceptions and observations, facts and metaphors, studies and history and lyricism all fit together, as it were, like hands joined.

Through this more holistic vision, we hope to communicate what is so dearly at stake should we continue to despoil our natural world. We are losing more than just beauty; we are losing our chance for physical and spiritual survival. Never before in history has there been a more urgent need to learn from nature, to take within us her beauty, wonder, and mystery. Environmental destruction imperils the planet. Greed and lies are at war with love and science. And yet what we need most is a fearless generosity and fierce hunger for truth, so that we have a chance to make this land once again our homeland.

The essays and poems in this book are love letters to the Sierra Nevada—to its bones of rock; to the clouds and glaciers and rivers and fires that have shaped it; to the living beings, large and small, who inhabit it. Our essays and poems are meditations on both the grandeur and the minutiae of the Sierra Nevada. This work arose through our direct experience, informed by our studies in science, natural history, poetry, and spirituality. How might study of the natural world illuminate the daily work of living and our responsibilities to the Earth and to each other? Through learning to see and know and love a singular place in its life-giving, wild, true reality, perhaps we might learn to see and know and love each place in the world for all its mystery and beauty. Perhaps we might arrest our calamitous way forward—and bend the arc of history to the invigorating work of healing what we can of the world's brokenness—for ourselves, for one another, and for the future. If we must walk holding grief in one hand, then let us walk holding hope in the other.

—RJN

THE PARADISE NOTEBOOKS

INTRODUCTION

We learn that there is a natural and inevitable conflict between science and spirituality; between the facts established by observation and experiment and those same facts shown in poetry, with its distinct and radiant spectrum of meaning. And this supposed conflict takes on acute form when our subject is the natural world. Can the earth be wholly understood as a set of elements configured by physical laws, and all life forms reduced definitively to a selection of random genetic variations from an original accident of organic chemistry?

Everyone, of course, must decide for themselves. But in the surround of beauties of the High Sierra, as we hiked, Richard and I talked not only of the elegant understanding of science but also of the countless declarations from the domain of spiritual writing, even in traditional and established faiths, that claim for nature a special place in spiritual practice. Witness these quotations, chosen nearly at random from around the world:

> The world originates so that truth may come and dwell therein.
> —Buddha

> If you would understand the invisible, look closely at the visible.
> —The Talmud

> Trees and stones will teach you that which you can never learn from any master.
> —Bernard of Clairvaux, Christian Saint

> Recognize what is in front of your face, and what is concealed from you will be revealed. For there is nothing hidden that will not be disclosed.
> —Jesus, The Gospel of Thomas

And in the shifting of the winds, and in the clouds that are pressed into service betwixt heaven and earth, are signs to people who can understand.

—The Koran

The sunlight becomes clear only if it can meet the light that is within us.

—Lao-Tse

Beyond these examples from widely practiced faiths, there is an abundance of texts in mysticism that testify to a life-giving dimension of meaning in nature. And then there are the offerings of poetry worldwide, which claim for nature a center-most place in our sense of beauty, of grace, of blessing, and of our whole hope for possibility and promise in our lives.

Richard and I wanted to bring these two worlds together: science and art, sense and spirit, quantity and quality, concept and metaphor. They belong together because they are one world, this world, where we live.

I have long been a devotee of natural history, with a special interest in the science of patterns. Yet such is the depth of nature—so potent and fabulous are her visitations and myriad beauties—that there has been no way to offer the story of my life with her, save by writing verse.

> We learn how, hidden in the mountain
> Among musical grasses, there is a fountain
>
> Of fine water moving irresistibly, a spring
> That is light made liquid, rising in rock
> That is foundation. Protection. A singing
>
> There has rhythm that answers a hunger
> With us always, and once in the wilderness
> When you heard it, you knew the address
> Of a sacred place. After downfall and anger,
>
> Soaring and failing, song and silence, you
> Know why it is shown to you: to unlock
> All the long beauties of the earth. For you
>
> Must be the rock where you stand,
> Learn how love takes form in land.

The story must be told in various forms—and most recently, since our trip to the Sierra, I have been visited by the chance to tell it in the concise form of haiku.

Mountain range—
How do you tend
Such infinitesimal flowers?

Mountain range—
Wakes up thinking:
Canyons, raptors, waterfalls.

Mountain range—
What's it like to be full
Of bluebirds and cougars?

Mountain range—
What's it like, the flash
Of so many rivers inside you?

Mountain range—
What's it like, the billion
Tree roots within you?

Mountain range—
What's it like, feeling
Every single snowflake?

Mountain range—
What's it like, to watch civilizations
Rise, then vanish?

Mountain range—
Is it exultation, the volcanoes,
Landslides, avalanches?

Mountain range—
Is it pure joy, to offer shelter
To cougar kittens?

Mountain range—
Every night, do you hope
To hear the owls?

Mountain range—
Can you feel the butterflies
Against your cheek?

Mountain range—
Do you love
Every single pine cone?

—SN

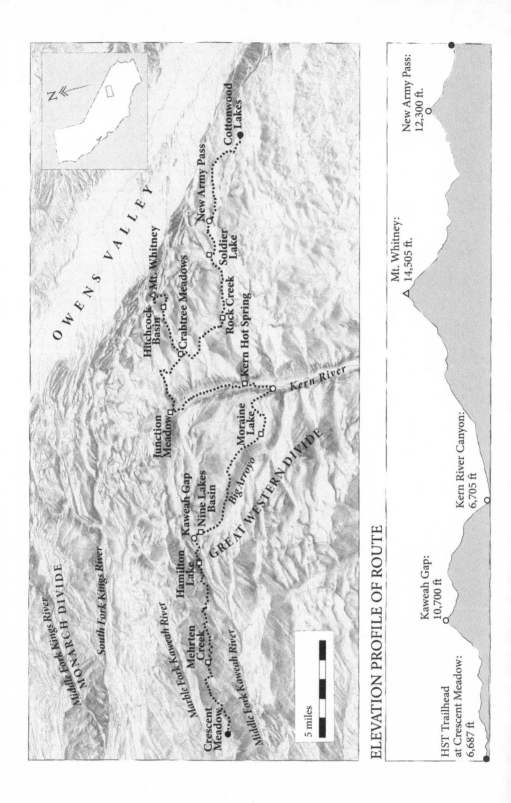

MONARCH DIVIDE

Middle Fork Kings River

South Fork Kings River

O W E N S   V A L L E Y

Hitchcock Basin

Mt. Whitney

Crabtree Meadows

New Army Pass

Cottonwood Lakes

Soldier Lake

Rock Creek

Kern Hot Spring

Junction Meadow

Kern River

Moraine Lake

Big Arroyo

GREAT WESTERN DIVIDE

Kaweah Gap

Nine Lakes Basin

Hamilton Lake

Marble Fork Kaweah River

Mehrten Creek

Middle Fork Kaweah River

Crescent Meadow

N

5 miles

ELEVATION PROFILE OF ROUTE

Mt. Whitney: 14,505 ft.

New Army Pass: 12,300 ft.

Kaweah Gap: 10,700 ft.

HST Trailhead at Crescent Meadow: 6,687 ft.

Kern River Canyon: 6,705 ft.

SETTING OUT

We were two families: Richard, his wife, Deborah, and their daughter, Sophie; Steven, his wife, Lucy, and their daughter, Gabriella. In the summer of 2017, we planned a hike through the High Sierra with the idea to traverse the whole range, west to east. To prepare for the trip, we read the accounts of those who preceded us on the trail and found alarmed posts about the dangerous currents in the creeks, their danger multiplied for us by our carrying heavy packs. And then there were stories of rattlesnake infestations in the lower elevations and even a photograph of a mountain lion lying in the middle of the trail. And we knew that, early in the trip, the climb to Kaweah Gap might require a crampon and ice ax traverse across a steep and icy snow chute.

But on August 3, we set out, and over the next thirteen days walked ninety miles. Beginning at Crescent Meadow in Sequoia National Park, the hike led us through big valleys, along the edges of precipitous canyons, over passes and around blue and silver high mountain lakes, to the summit of Mount Whitney; through brilliant green meadows and by the sides of creeks that, because of the big winter, had become torrents. Our destination would be Cottonwood Lakes in the Golden Trout Wilderness, on the eastern side of the Sierra, looking east over the Great Basin.

Our daughters were close friends, both sixteen years old, and followed the trail with the speed and grace of gazelles. The rest of us strode along in their slipstream.

Our journey across the range was more than an excursion through terrain filled with resurgent wildness. It was a vanishing into beauty, in which our lives were re-created from within by the power of the mountains—beckoning, forthright, irresistible.

STONE, FIRE, WATER

The essential thing is to become again the light vagabonds of the earth.

—Jean Giono

GRANITE

With hope one can do anything. And the mountains that one causes to arise are real flesh-and-blood mountains and the trees are at home on them and the streams sleep on beds of granite as clean as golden corn.

—Jean Giono

Passive—as Granite—laps my music—

—Emily Dickinson

8/3/17, Day 1. Up at 3 am, anxious. Feels like pre-race jitters. Big breakfast at the lodge at Cedar Grove. Last real coffee for two weeks. Skies overcast, humid at the trailhead. Thank God, moving at last. Afternoon splinters of lightning and cracks and booms of thunder. Reached a creek that was raging fast and had to scoot over a log bridge. Sketchy. Lush, lush, lush along the trail. Wildflowers everywhere. Ferns and elder-berry. Fireweed, different species of paintbrush, sneezeweed, pale blooms of tincture plant, sprays of groundsmoke, little eriogonums.

Granite is the geologic backbone of the Sierra Nevada. The great spine of rock holds diverse forests, dreamy meadows, skeins of streams, radiant lakes, and rare glaciers. Life ascends even to the highest reaches of the range, thousands of feet above tree line, where gardens of black, orange, and chartreuse lichen adorn the rock. Everywhere a tenacious living skin sheaths the ancient bones of the mountains. But this choice of metaphor—life as skin—is one shaped, like so much of our under-standing about the universe, by a particular, human, limited experience of time.

Imagine, for a moment, if we could peer through a lens that sped up time so that centuries hurtled by in seconds. Trees would leap into the sky as they snaked their roots into fissures, wedging and prying apart the granite. Lichens would spread across the rock, enlivening its surface with colorful splotches, secreting caustic acids, and digesting minerals. Exposed to such vigorous and irrepressible activity, stone monuments would decompose over the course of a few, brief, time-warped days into humble soil. From the rock's perspective, this so-called living skin might seem more invasion than ornament.

If our lens allowed time to race by even faster, whole eons drifting by in hours, we would learn that granite is a product of life, a rock unique to Earth, made possible by photosynthesis. The discovery of photosynthesis by primitive microorganisms had consequences: it transformed Earth's early atmosphere into an oxygenated, caustic pall that could weather rocks into dust with unprecedented efficiency. Dust is where granite begins. Such dust settles on the seafloor in thick, spongy blankets of sediment whose pores cumulatively hold small oceans of water, which with time is bound to minerals as sediment hardens first to sedimentary rock.

Then, where dense slabs of seafloor rock plunge into the Earth's scalding inte-rior, dragging their sedimentary blankets and metamorphosed beds along for the ride, water is baked out and released into the overlying mantle. The flux of water eases the mantle's melting, giving rise to glowing, buoyant pods of magma that push up against and crack the rocks above. The magma ascends, penetrates the crust, ingests slivers of the crustal rock, and takes on the composition of granite before cooling and crystallizing into stone. It is in this way, from the seeds of dust, that granite emerges into the world.

Bodies of solid granite, when with time they rise to the surface by the action of tectonic events or slow mantle churnings, make great spines of mountains like the Sierra Nevada. The mountains heave miles up into the clouds, and life takes hold. Each living thing finds its place to thrive—the oak, the bear, the green bottle fly, the ruby-barked red fir too. Even among the highest peaks, the gray-crowned rosy-finch, the bighorn sheep, the pika, and the skypilot with its violet-cobalt blooms make their home among the enchanted stone that air and dust and time and life made possible.

—RJN

We might ask, as we look at any landscape, how its history resembles a land we carry within. Walking among the granite peaks, over the lichen, near the black bear, close to the marmot and among the meadows, we came slowly to understand that the whole Sierra is a most unlikely gift. In the sweep of time, it is a gift made just now, just here; a gift with the power to awaken us to our chance to watch and listen.

Sometimes the land turns into words; sometimes into proverbs.

As we hiked, what we saw—pines and oaks, grasses and lilies, coyotes and golden trout, root fungus and moss and the grace of deer—was just the beginning of what was before us. It was, and is, to the reality of the Sierra what the skin of a peach is to a peach; what the flashing of light on the surface of a river is to the whole surging river; what the first paragraphs of a beautiful book are to the finished and intricate story within.

This is true for everyone, wherever we are: what we see is the preface to what we can see. Beyond that preface, with work and love, is what we can come to understand.

If we can understand, then we can live.

In the Sierra, we understood that we might, after all, belong here with tree and rock and time and light. We might, for a brief spell of years, have the luck to find a home here by following the beauty that beckons us. We are spellbound here.

Thoreau wrote, in the last sentence of his book about life in a cabin alongside Walden pond, "The sun is but a morning star." The thirteenth-century poet Rumi wrote, "As soon as you entered this world of forms, an escape ladder was put out for you." Emily Dickinson wrote, "This world is not conclusion."

If we are to follow such declarations, we have to immerse ourselves in this world, so as to find our way through to the deep reality of another world held within this one. It is as if the earth is complete unto itself, and yet a gorgeous portal. It is as if, over a long period of study, we must dissolve ourselves. In just the same way that oxygen was an agent of change, because of its toxic power, so the clarity we come to will break down the person we have constructed, who stands between us and reality. Once that dissolution has happened, then we can await the heat and pressure and movement, the patient re-creation of ourselves, until one day in the sunlight we learn that our lives can hold oak and bear, green bottle fly and rough-hewn ridgeline. We can learn how a place we love composes us. We can work and live to honor the symposium of the whole.

Is it possible that we are unified, body and mind, with this earth, and the life it offers? That books are nature, and that we can walk across a beautiful meadow, even in our own houses? Is it possible that there is, in rock, a plainly offered paradise?

It's true, there's a wildcat in the pantry,
Falcons in your hat. To live wide and free

In this homely destination of soul, means
That we are here, friends, together, talking
In the sunlight as twenty antelope careen

Around the table, as from the next room
We hear books cartwheeling off the shelves,
Novels opening, women standing, themselves
At last, transfigured at last—whatever doom

Or triumph they suffered in their story, now
They set aside, for a chance to be walking
Curiously through a meadow, as the oaks bow

Before bullsnake, honeybee, and peacock,
Before paradise irrepressible in plain rock.

—SN

OBSIDIAN

Obsidian is so sharp that you can use it to cut your lousy life to pieces, and then when you have the original parts, the real ones, you can put them back together and have a clean assembly of things and see the world as it is and always was, and get to work at last, before it's too goddam late.

—A Nevada hermit living near Big Smokey Valley

8/4/17, Day 2. Up too early again. Listening to the patter of rain dripping from the tree limbs onto the tent and the hush of the creek in the darkness. Breathing in the scent of earth and rain. I can't believe we are here, surrounded by these old trees and mountains, with days ahead of us. I'm a little boy all over again, incredulous that this place actually exists, and I am here in it. I want to get up and wander down to the creek and feel its black, wet, cold aliveness on my skin. But it's so warm in this sleeping bag.

Running south of the turquoise eye of Mono Lake just east of the Sierra's steep escarpment there are hills that once hissed and groaned, gushed fountains of pumice and ash and sticky masses of incandescent lava. Today, wandering among the range of stubby volcanic hills leads you across piles of pumice that grind and crunch underfoot. Daliesque spires of black, lichen-spotted obsidian tilt like disfigured statues at strange angles into the sky.

It is a land of glass, a land fashioned during recent millennia from obsidian and pumice with the same chemical composition as granite. But there the similarities with granite end. The granitic rocks of the Sierra formed on the order of a hundred million years ago, whereas the obsidian craters just east of the range erupted in the last few millennia, some in recent centuries. Furthermore, making granite requires time enough for melt to cool slowly in the insulating warmth of earth's crust, enough time to allow for myriad atoms vibrating within it to arrange themselves into proper crystals. No such leisure exists for melt that erupts at the surface. It is granite flash-frozen. It is a chaos, a pandemonium contained in stone.

Imagine you are small, so small that could you enter the strange world within a shard of obsidian. You would enter into a world of buzzing atoms—iron, magnesium, aluminum, calcium, sodium, and potassium spun out among tumultuous arrangements of silicon and oxygen. If only given more time, these atoms would have ordered themselves into the neat, patterned, geometric symmetry of crystals. Yet it is the pure, unbridled disorder of obsidian that makes it so extraordinary. When granite breaks, it cleaves along rough, ragged surfaces defined by boundaries between crystals and planes of molecular weakness within its constituent minerals. This interior order guides fractures and limits the acuteness of edges made by their intersections. It is different with obsidian.

Consider by way of analogy two chocolate bars: one with a pattern of small squares impressed upon it, the other just a simple, unscored, uniform bar. When pressure is applied to each, the first will tend to break into little squares, but the second will break haphazardly into sharp-edged fragments. Obsidian, because it lacks the constraints imposed by an internal molecular order, can in fact be flaked into tools with edges that are many times sharper than a razor blade. For this reason, volcanic glass, rather than surgical steel, is the material of choice for scalpels used by some plastic surgeons.

In the Sierra Nevada, we find flakes of obsidian, shards left by indigenous hunters who worked the black volcanic glass into arrowpoints, their edges sharpened to translucence, to hunt the animals that would sustain their loved ones. Throughout their millennia of continuous presence in the Mono Basin, they would have witnessed volcanic eruptions give birth to the region's pale hills. What stories did they tell, these hunters and their kin, on dark summer nights as they gazed upon the cradling arms of the Milky Way, of how the stone that took life and gave life came itself into life? What stories have we remembered?

—RJN

What if it were true that our capacities of mind have a direct relation to the workings of earth? That there is some deep resemblance between the making of a mountain and the making of a mind?

Some of our capacities—reason, mathematical thinking, logic—need gradual maturation and a slow coming to order. We set aside and assemble in our minds the elements of a problem, and then take the time to draw out the pattern, the natural and fitting order that brings all those elements beautifully together. True granite needs the protection of the earth's crust to allow time for silicon and oxygen and myriad other elements, with minute coordination, to make precisely configured crystals. And in our lives, we need the protection of peace and a concentration of labors to find our way into a finery of order that awaits in the mind.

But other capacities we have—intuition, fresh insight, conceptual breakthroughs, transcendental understandings—can come into creation swiftly. It is as if to take form they need to be given directly into light and air; that is, into the living world. Just as molten rock was released onto the land around Mono Lake, we must bring our unformed, necessary ideas into the open and ready world. There, rather than falling into a fixed and beautiful order, on occasion our ideas alter strangely and fall into a supple and miraculous disorder. And what we might hope for then is unprecedented sharpness of mind, a body of thought that even when broken shows edges of fine and effective power. It is a power more than human: our collaboration with the earth, so that we may become useful to the time and place we live. We can do so because the sharpness we have is one we can use to hunt a sustenance of mind that we then can share; that we then can give away to anyone who is ready to receive it.

And more than that: in the encounter with light and air, some of our meditations can be sewn through with pockets of air that give buoyancy to the workings of our minds. Just as a pumice stone is made of glass and air, so the mind, working in concord with the earth, lives in miraculous contradiction: sometimes fiercely sharp as obsidian, sometimes soft and yielding like pumice. We may work with the world's best cutting tool. Or we may make strange magic: pumice is the only stone that floats.

Everything that we call miraculous is an artful variation in the order of mind and nature. When it is made in the natural world, we can come to understand it. When it is made by the mind, we can learn from it, and come home to earth. Shabistari wrote, "Your body is like earth and your head the sky. Your bones are like mountains, rough and hard. Vegetation is your hair and trees are your limbs."

What is this state of mind? It has joy and memory and unity. It has liberation and a departure from ourselves, and then a re-creation of ourselves.

> Mind is stone and light, river, comet,
> Trust and story, gut, sun, sonnet,
>
> Stageset of centuries, ship whose sails
> Catch trade winds of time, to search
> For your work. Leave behind buried jails
>
> Of everything you have been ever,
> And ride the wild horse of the sun,
> Hoof beats like heartbeats, joy undone
> And made as you wander and suffer,
>
> As you answer and you remember . . .

—SN

ROOF PENDANTS

As for the earth, out of it comes bread; but underneath it is turned up by fire. Its stones are the place of sapphires, and it has dust of gold.

—The Book of Job

Even though most of the metamorphic rocks in the central Sierra have been uplifted and eroded away, those remaining tell an important story about the earliest history of the region. The story is difficult to read, however, because of the brutal processes that have affected these rocks since their deposition.

—James G. Moore

8/4/17, Day 2. Overcast, damp morning. Views of the glacier-chiseled face of the Great Western Divide between fat red firs sleeved in wolf lichen. Crossed a wooden bridge over the gorge shot through by Lone Pine Creek, then switchbacked up a granite shoulder before contouring back toward Hamilton Lakes Basin. Set up our tents among lodgepole pine groves, near a slab of granite overlooking the water. Watched a rainbow arcing across the peaks of the Divide, waterfalls braiding down dark cliffs. Cold baths for all.

Gazing out across the roof of the Sierra Nevada, one might spy thin black and rust-orange fins of frost-heaved metamorphic rock riding atop bright granite. These fins, known as roof pendants, were travelers once, geologic migrants from the sea. They are scraps of balmy archipelagos and a once vibrant seabed that lay beneath them. They journeyed across the great Panthalassic Ocean, ancestor of the Pacific, ferried aboard a tectonic plate that slid eastward until it encountered western North America. For more than a hundred million years this plate, the Farallon Plate, pulled by its immense, dense mass, bent where it met the continent and descended into the mantle's scorching interior. Some slivers of seafloor and islands managed to escape, scraped off like skin against the continent's edge. With each new addition of some island or welt of oceanic rock to the continental boundary, North America expanded westward in a kind of geologic manifest destiny. Bodies of granitic magma swarmed the scraped-off seafaring migrants, and transfigured them once again with ferocious heat and pressure. In the last few millions of years, the amalgam of deformed exotic rocks has risen miles into the sky, even as the range has been given line and shape and texture by glaciers and rivers.

Today the maritime origin of the Sierra roof pendants—the remains of plankton, or coral reefs, or submarine lava flows, or of seabed sediments made from fragments of much older mountains—is hardly recognizable. Once horizontal layers of seafloor sediment are now accordioned. The delicate edifices of coral reefs have recrystallized into mosaics of scintillant calcite, revealed in Sierra caverns. Elsewhere, the ancient seabed, where it lies adjacent to the granite, has been swirled like taffy, transformed into assemblages of blood-red garnet, ebony hornblende, glittering varieties of mica, and many other minerals. Some of the pendants' iron-rich minerals rust into oxides, and where abundant they stain the rock to rich shades of umber and chocolate. Such mineral stains occasionally reveal deposits of dispersed gold, silver, tungsten, copper, and other valuable metals that formed when superheated, mineral-charged waters escaped from crystallizing granite and reacted with the seafloor remnants.

But there is an even rarer treasure among the high country roof pendants. The distinctive chemical compositions of these geologic travelers give rise to thin scrapes of distinctive soils. Such soils, in the austere climatic conditions of high elevation, nurture gardens with delicate wildflowers you will not find blossoming elsewhere in the Sierra—such as the curiously erotic lavender blooms of Parry's oxytrope, sleeved in their wooly sepals, and the veined, translucent petals of the small-flowered grass of Parnassus. Into these Sierra flower gardens wander bees and butterflies and hummingbirds. Alpine chipmunks burrow underneath as the shape of a falcon hurtles overhead. Life is a journeywork; life turns to life.

—RJN

So many, in so many ways, have found in poetry a way forward for the mind and spirit. When we look at how this might be, we return inevitably to inquire about the nature of beauty.

In most cultures, in every century, beauty is bound up with unity. Beauty illuminates the affinity, the inner relation, the resemblance, the kinship, the concord and identity of things. We are all trained to tell things apart. In the experience of beauty, we learn to tell things alike; to move from the darkness of oneself to a sympathy, an open rapport; a longed-for, conscious union with the world. Beauty is a lucid and graceful assembly of forms that calls the mind close to life, our bodies close to the earth, and all of us closer to one another.

We strive for such an assembly, no matter the cost to ourselves; no matter how much we must disappear into the work.

Think of the tectonic plates whose movement carried those islands and reefs across the ocean, until at last most of them disappeared beneath the western edge of North America. Yet some portions survived the journey. What once was cooled by trade winds now is undone and re-created. With the rising of the Sierra Nevada and the revealing work of wind and ice, the material rises again, metamorphosed, into the sunlight. This is the world of resemblance, as in the view of the Zuni: "The sun, moon, and the stars, the sky, earth, and sea, in all their phenomena and elements; and all inanimate objects, as well as plants, animals, and men . . . belong to one great system of all-conscious and interrelated life, in which the degrees of relationship seem to be determined largely, if not wholly, by the degrees of resemblance."

Mountains are oceans. Over the pass, you may find an island illuminated. On the top of a marble butte in winter, you may be in the tropics. The pastel beauties of coral may be found in hard stone in a dark cave. A passage through once molten rock may make the soil that bears the flower that brings the hummingbird.

In any one place may be held all places. One beauty gathers into itself other beauties. Each world bears all the worlds we might find within it. If you understand one outcropping of stone, or one wildflower, or one hummingbird—if we see our way along the tracery of cause and effect, the mystery of change and re-creation—then we are led to everything we see, and everything we are. The earth is inclusive. It includes us, teaching us how we must be re-created by the heat and movement over years of our love and understanding. We ourselves change as we step aside from our practical affairs and give ourselves over, wholly and irrevocably, to the beauties of earth. By such loving, we take on another life, as surely as ancient seafloor and islands turn into the glittering mineral pendants of the Sierra Nevada.

> When you do not match your likeness, your
> Profile changes like the cloud edge, the shore
> You are is formed by the waves you make;
> When you stand forth and let wind shake
>
> A soul from your flesh, and wings of vision
> You visit on the body of your sight; your days
> You rescue in midair, from a gear train driven
> By your career in time; you draw your face
>
> Over again, according to prophecy, learn then
> Your voice is not yours, that what is drawn
> Is death worth having; and that in the song
> For one you love you lose your words, when
>
> You are made over, according to love and her lineage,
> In the likeness of all the earth, in her moving image.

—SN

BROKENNESS

Pain is a treasure, for it contains mercies.
The kernel is soft when the rind is scraped off.
O friend, the place of darkness and cold
Is the fountain of life and the cup of ecstasy.

—Jalaludin Rumi

When you find life you will know
that even the mineral world is alive.

—Shabistari

Finding beauty in a broken world is creating beauty in the world we find.

—Terry Tempest Williams

8/5/17, Day 3. Morning of fear. In an hour, we'll begin the 2,400-foot climb to Kaweah Gap and into Nine Lakes Basin with packs still heavy. Pools of rainwater have collected overnight in shallow bowls in the granite. Doe browsing with her fawn near camp. Passed through the rock tunnel. Smell of earth, rock, and rain. Wildflowers, wild onions. Crampons on boots, went up the long shoot of watermelon snow— made it to the Gap, wind and clouds whipping around us. Found a campsite in an island of low scattered foxtails near a rush of water in the basin of Big Arroyo. Surrounded by granite with shoulders of chocolate and rust colored metamorphic roof pendants of Lawson Peak, Kaweah Queen, and Black Kaweah. Lightning and thunder all afternoon.

Walking in the high country of the Sierra Nevada, I see it is broken everywhere. This is especially apparent in the crumbling choss piles mantling the mountaintops, where the rock is heaved apart by snowmelt that trickles down into hard cracks and freezes there in the brittle darkness of night. The rock is rent by nothing more than the silent and invisible pirouetting of water molecules arranging themselves into hexagon shaped crystals that bend stone until it shatters like a beer bottle left too long in the freezer. Such a tiny thing is water, this breaker of mountains.

Climb a broken bricolage of talus. Ascend with a saint's patience as you navigate each uneasy truce of friction and gravity. Rocks seesaw and whine as you step. They rasp and grind like anxious teeth, the scent of breaking minerals prickling the air like gunpowder. The whole loose mountainside waits on edge, waits for one lever of stone that will send it all roiling down, smashing rock to dust, crushing your body. Or maybe you might just turn your ankle and hobble back to camp, pelted and pummeled by hail. But look carefully; there are small graces everywhere. Among the fractured heaps of granite are thin scrims of mineral soil holding pincushion plants with their succulent leaves furred in fine silver and whose flowers stare you down and beckon you with all their seductiveness to come to them. With gentle footsteps you trace each riven scar in stone, each narrow borderland of destruction and possibility.

Look up from this bald granite country you are wandering across, up from the blazing brightness of the speckled white and black and silvery minerals, up to the sheer precipices of granite that, although intact enough to hold themselves up, are everywhere riven with cracks. Geologists call them joints, these narrow slits in stone, which is a strange name given that they note where the rock is doing the opposite of joining. Joints are where the strength of rock has yielded; where it has given in, cleaved from itself, come unhinged. Everywhere you look the mountains are crazed with cracks. Everywhere you look the world is broken.

Geologists have described whole families of joints cutting through the granites of the Sierra Nevada, running through the rock like the grain of split lumber. Some joints formed soon after the granite crystallized from melt and mineral slushes in glowing wombs deep below the surface. The rock cooled, contracted, and fractured deep in the earth's blackness. Water heated to eight hundred degrees Fahrenheit trickled through slim passages in the stone, reacting with the granite and filling the cracks with seams of glinting green minerals. In places you can see where the old wounds have opened to reveal their crystal-crusted faces, sparkling with a pistachio and emerald-black glitter.

Some joints are stretch marks, traces of breakage under tension. They split the Sierra into sheets of stone. They parallel the Sierra's steep eastern escarpment— and as well the mountainous slivers of the Basin and Range inching skyward from the taut earth. Another family of joints, paralleling the San Andreas Fault, has crept into the Sierra as the Pacific Plate has sheared the western edge of North America into a splintered wreckage. And another family of joints formed as the Sierra ascended to the surface while the rock above was rasped away by rivers and ice. Heaps of jumbled stone slid down the mountainsides in brutal avalanches. The unburdening of the Range of Light enabled the underlying granite to expand to the point of breaking along great curving fissures. And the land is breaking now, all about us. Networks of cracks wander across the rock, race up sheer cliffs of granite honed to knives' edges by glaciers. Brokenness makes a mosaic of the land.

Throughout the granite's interior, where it is still unbroken and intact, it is as purely sterile and lightless as at its moment of crystallization into stone-being. But when the granite yields in a seismic spasm, breaking at the surface, it reveals itself for the first time in its hundred-million-year-old history. There is no going back. The rock exposes its darkness to the world, lays itself bare to receive long-journeying photons from distant stars; the caressing hushes and howling of wind; the prying claws of ice; the dawn choruses of birds; the snowy solstices of winter; seeds, spores, and microorganismic universes of inchoate alpine soil; miniature Zen gardens of orange and black and gray and chartreuse lichens digesting the rock surface; the anxious, insistent scratching of rodentine paws. The families of fractures are the dark interior passages through which foil-thin films of water seep through the Sierra's granite backbone. They are the great lineaments of the range along which seeds find refuge, set roots, and make a go of it, probing with thin fingers down in darkness to auger for what water they might find. These cracks are the broken places where colonies of bats might roost, a pair of peregrine falcons might build a nest, where we might take shelter from a passing summer shower. Joints are where the granite lays itself bare to the widening heaven and the inevitable ruin that breaking brings.

Trace the scars in the palm of your hand, or the furrows in the broken recti-
linear array of bark sheathing a western white pine, or the curving crevasses of a
Sierra glacier; for everywhere we look the world is broken. To wonder why bro-
kenness exists is to wonder why things are at all. To exist in this world, to know
this world, is to be made from one's first days broken, permeable, naked—exposed
to dark trickling waters that seek a way through the fractured, silent underworld
of the stone that is us.

—RJN

It was a daunting contemplation, when we stood back before our hike to look
toward the jagged peaks, shattered archways, rockslides, flying canyons, teeter-
ing boulders, clamorous rivers, and glinting high granite of the Sierra Nevada. It
looked whole, impassable, and complete unto itself, as if it dwelt in some blessed,
fateful, and separate world.

But then it was time to set out, and for thirteen days we traced our way along
the contours of rock cut by rivers, or straight up canyon walls via improbable and
perilous switchbacks, or along slanted, hard-packed snow with crampons, on the
way up to freezing high passes. Our daughters floated off far ahead of us, as if they
had made some secret deal with gravity, who loved them, and let them go weight-
lessly along.

We learned how the mountains are whole and beautiful for one principal rea-
son: they have been broken so often. It is a teaching story, and it gives us a per-
spective for our own lives: for all of us are broken by history, which can seem at
times like a malignant force. Look at the bare record: slavery, war, contempt for
women, the savageries of politics that have left centuries disfigured by one mass
extermination after another; the way wealth seems to mutilate conscience, the
shameful persistence of racism and ethnic loathing; and in our own times the
progressive destruction of the biosphere, a destruction that would take most of
us down with it.

As we learn what we have done—what we do to one another and to life on
earth—the knowledge seeps into us along fissures, and myriad breakages and
cleavings open within us because of sorrow, the study of history, our own ruinous
heartbreaks, the suffering of injustice and oppression, and the militant economic
assault upon the life of the earth. It is a cumulative aggression so severe and mer-
ciless, it might be called demonic.

Because of such learning, most of us have times when we awaken ransacked by
disbelief and despair. Yet the Sierra Nevada teaches us the central lesson we need.
It is the very breaking and jointing, the cracking and carving and breakdown, the

weathering and scouring, that all together give rise to the countless forms of beauty—iridescent, miraculous, gift-giving, exultant—throughout the whole of the range.

We are all broken. It is how room is made within us for the world to take root. We can, with work and luck, yield ourselves in favor of the healing, potent, mantic offerings of life all around us at every minute.

> One day, could the earth come round
> To you, around you, within you?
>
> Alive and enticing and simmering with ideas,
> Eccentricities, textures, experiments?
>
> So that you are fully inhabited?
>
> So that you are empty at last of yourself, but
> Rambunctiously full of world?
>
> Rivers run down your veins, stars
> Form in your sweat?
>
> Your ideas gleam in river currents
> Rampaging down the granite canyons?
>
> Your hands know how to weave
> All sunlight through a single pine?
>
> All your joy comes together
> In favor of a journeywork await within you?
>
> Because you must travel to the source of all winds,
> The headwaters of all rivers?
>
> The meeting ground of all oceans, the mountains
> Whose words are wellspring of all dreams?
>
> Travel to the place where the earth, one morning,
> First thought of wings?
>
> The place where the first dance was danced,
> The first poetry was born in foretold rapture?

Will you visit the cynosure of light?

So that when night comes you can
Enfold the moon in your arms?

And you can sing to her, as you have always
Sung to her?

And the next day, have the chance to be as useful
As a single feather in a falcon's wing?

Have the chance to learn from the mockingbird
The songs of all the musicians of the earth?

Have the chance to give away every minute
Of your life?

Have the chance to love?

—SN

CLOUDS

. . . Great clouds—like Ushers—leaning—
Creation—looking on—

. . . Two Worlds—like Audiences—disperse—
And Leave the Soul—alone.

—Emily Dickinson

8/5/17, Day 3, PM. Rainy, cold afternoon. Passed out in the tent until Sophie woke me because a ranger wanted to talk. He had just rescued two teenaged boys on the Kaweah Crest who didn't have proper gear or even a stove (but still had an emergency beacon!). How the fuck did they even get up there? They could well have died, and the ranger asked us to watch after them until the morning. We gave the boys warm food and hot chocolate. Felt sorry for the younger skinny kid who looked like a wet noodle that could have slipped through a colander in his goddamned tennis shoes. Seriously?

By mid-morning the sun has shouldered up into the blue east. Serrated ridges rise like an archipelago from the forest. Peaks warm, send plumes of air lofting skyward. Air ascends, cools, and expands, condensing wisps of cottony cloud. A single cloud stretches and floats, turns like a cat in mid-air. It shape-shifts, bends, feints with a paw.

Within an hour the sky has assembled a menagerie of them. A raven, horse, hummingbird, coyote, jackrabbit, a grinning bear, an improbable anteater, an even more improbable mammoth. The clouds parade above the tree-bare peaks. Their bellies swell with gray shadow. They float and turn and slow-dance. Yesterday all of it was blue, empty, this sky; aching, alone, and still as stone, as blue as the fire of stars. But here, now, on this morning, shadows of cloud drift across the mountains' sleepy faces.

In the Sierra, in the warm days of July and August, a summer rainstorm might arrive most any afternoon, blossoming from moist masses of air inhaled from California's interior, drawn inward and upward into the range. It's hard to know what might happen in a day of high mountain wandering. It's best you come prepared.

By midday the clouds billow. They push high and hard into the blue, rising, mountains above mountains. Morning stretches to afternoon. An assembly of clouds masses over ranges to the east. Clouds ascend; sprout puffy bouffants; churn and roil into high, frigid air; wisp out silky, frozen strands as each begins an electrical transformation into a voluminous battery.

How does this happen? A cloud is a gathering of mist, trillions of droplets of water, each droplet the size of a corpuscle of blood. As a cloud droplet cools, its liquid chaos comes to order, assembling into crystalline ice. Freezing subdues liquid water's ecstatic molecular dance to a gentle thrum as the water sheds heat—the latent heat of crystallization—to the surrounding air of the cloud. Multiplied over trillions of times, heat radiated from the freezing of each tiny globe of water warms the cloud, livening it with renewed buoyancy, sending it higher into the cobalt sky.

The cloud hauls its immense mass of water upward. Tons of it. Water contained within a modest cumulus cloud might weigh as much as few bison. The water in a towering thunderhead might weigh as much as a herd of them, one million strong. A raincloud is a river of bison running up into the sky. The cloud rises until it reaches the base of the stratosphere and sprawls out, a stampede turning at an invisible wall.

Freezing droplets of mist in the upper reaches of the cloud explode into glinting ice flecks. Riding on roller-coastering currents, crystal shards of ice tumble through the air and collide with supercooled droplets of liquid water—water that is chilled far below the freezing point without actually freezing. The supercooled droplets freeze instantaneously on contact with the ice crystals, sheathing the crystals in hoary coats of rime, plumping them to frothy spheres called graupel. Once an orb of graupel gains sufficient heft, it plummets down through the cloud. Hordes of falling graupel push cold gusts of wind downward, and send them rushing over the mountains below—breaths of cold air that warn of the electrical metamorphosis now well underway in the cloud.

Electrification occurs as collisions between graupel and snow shear loosely bound electrons from snow crystals and transfer them to the more massive spheres of graupel. In the melee graupel accumulates negative electrical charge and snowflakes acquire positive electrical charge. The snowflakes ride upward on buoyant air currents, causing positive electrical charge to concentrate toward the top of the cloud, while the gravity-driven downward movement of graupel concentrates negative charge in the cloud's belly.

All of this flurrying activity—from the moment a cloud's droplets of mist first begin to freeze, to the precipitation of graupel, and finally to the electrification of the cloud—might take no more than half an hour. The segregation of the cloud into oppositely charged regions, separated by a barrier of several thousand feet, cannot be sustained. Opposites attract. Attraction overwhelms. For this and so many other reasons, a Sierra mountain wanderer would be wise to attend to the movement of clouds.

How much energy does it take to lift a mass of water weighing as much as a herd of bison miles into the sky? How much does it take to lift a cloud? How many elevators running full-bore day and night? A bolt of lightning contains a tiny fraction of this energy, but transformed and concentrated into electricity. A glowing electric vein of lightning, perhaps no wider than the wrist of a child, is hotter than the surface of the sun, powerful enough to blast the bark off a tree, fuse rock to glass, end the drumming of a heart within its fragile cage of bone.

So many summer afternoons when I've wandered the Sierra, rainclouds have gathered above me, unfolding like the blossoming of dark irises. They rumble and boom and clap, send me scrambling in fear and fill me with a bewildering joy just to be alive among mountains and clouds and rain and thunder and lightning. The sky cracks open, thunder reverberates down canyons and over mountaintops, the echoing revealing the land's form and contour. From the earth rises an incense of petrichor, a musk of stone and ice and astringent mountain herbs. Lightning skitters within clouds and from clouds to mountaintops, ignites a high, lone bole that starts smoldering as rain and hail tumble from the sky. Almost too soon the storm lifts and is gone. The clouds wisp to gauze, the blue sky returns, the streams run full over stones.

—RJN

The writer Jorge Luis Borges, a profoundly inventive poet and storyteller, once gave an interview in which he downplayed the value of invention itself. He suggested that to invent a new form or style has some limited value, but the great thing, the difficult thing, is just to see what is right in front of us.

We see clouds every day . . . or do we? What if we were to take the time and observe them slowly and devotedly, to watch their gentle, inevitable, traveling work in the world? What if we might live for a spell of time as students of their beauty and their movement, the cadence of their change, and their daily, miraculous role on the whole stage of nature? What if we were to take instruction from cirrus, or attend the school of cumulus?

It is a contemplation both head-spinning and life-giving. Whence comes the water vapor that composes a cloud? From all the earth and its life: rivers and lakes, from the ocean and forest ponds, from our sweat, the moisture in our breath, from melting ice and the countless drops of dew that, in the warmth of the morning, offer a script of light across every Sierra meadow. The vapor rises invisibly into the light and becomes visible with slow beauty. This play of luminosity and presence brings to mind the established definition of sacrament: the outward and visible sign of an inward and invisible grace.

And how does such grace show itself? We need only look skyward. There is a rambunctious, unbound spirit at work. In a spell of days we will see a whole, supple, miraculous spectrum of cloud-forms—from noctilucent to stratus to lenticular. And all this is just preparation. The water called forth from the earth is assembled, readied, and returned faithfully to all of us. We are delivered a promiscuous variety of gifts: mist, fog, downpours, sleet, hail, snow, the squall and the tempest, the blizzard and the booming of thunder, the showtime of lightning and the lilting of soft rain.

Clouds are an invitation to bear witness to the unity of earth and sky; an invitation to unify our own lives with the workings of the earth. They show us the principle that must be central to our days: what is taken must be given. It is a dynamic and beautiful lesson in generosity and conduct. We die within, and the earth dies around us, if we do not honor that lesson.

Clouds are present every day, our sidekicks, friends, benefactors and professors. Can we learn from them?

> Clouds, teach me
> Internal readiness for
> The heavenly winds.

> Clouds, teach me
> How to darken ferociously,
> Then give soft living rain.

> Clouds, teach me
> To be an ebullient, spectral,
> Playful shape-shifter.

> Clouds, teach me
> To loosen and be combed
> By light across the sky.

> Clouds, teach me
> How to hold pale soft lush
> Golden light at morning.

> Clouds, teach me
> Thunder, climactic release
> Cracking with joy.

> Clouds, teach me
> Lightning, to walk in radiance
> Across the face of the earth.

> Clouds, teach me
> The slow crimson gliding
> Through late twilight.

Clouds, teach me
To make secretly in winter
   A billion floating jewels.

Clouds, teach me
Your tryst with air—supple,
   Responsive, erotic.

Clouds, teach me
To stand up, and reach
   For the azure zenith.

Clouds, teach me
The concerto you make
   With hail on a metal roof.

Clouds, teach me
To rise secretly from earth,
   To return full of clear life.

Clouds, teach me—
One day a wisp, tomorrow
   The whole of the sky.

Clouds, teach me
The cut-loose love
   Of long warm shining rain.

                              —SN

SNOW

I must say the maker of the world exhausts his skill with each snowflake and dewdrop that he sends down. We think that one mechanically coheres and that the other simply flows together and falls, but in truth they are the product of enthusiasm, the children of an ecstasy. . . .

—Thoreau

8/6/17, Day 4. Nine Lakes Basin, following Big Arroyo to Chagoopa Plateau and Moraine Lake. Deb woke up with a horrendous migraine like an axe through her forehead. Not a good way to start, but she willed herself to life and through the morning walked silently, hanging back. She is my badass. The rain cleared, a bluebird day. Crisscrossed back and forth over Big Arroyo, fording the shallows where it runs over smooth granite, then started a climb through twisting lodgepoles and foxtails to Chagoopa. Steve, walking along at top speed, the brim of his cap pulled down, smacked straight into a branch that extended across the trail at just the height of his forehead. Sounded like a gunshot, and he crumpled to the ground. Evac options racing through my head. Then he's slowly upright, says he briefly visited interstellar space. No actual brain damage, or so it would seem. We'll see if it scrambles his haiku. Rattlesnake in the tumbledown logs by the lake, need to be careful. Scared. Beautiful, terrifying. Nightmare stuff.

In late autumn the Pacific Ocean spawns great spiraling storms. They inhale the sea, haul out to shore, and vault up the canyoned ramp of the Sierra. Up in the mountains, the sky waits. An atmospheric halo of ice crystals encircles the sun. The air conjures a steely mineral scent, prickles against your skin. The sky goes galvanic. Clouds soften. The world says snow. Snowflakes float and twirl from the clouds. Cold crystals of snow dust your eyelashes, collect on your gloves.

With the aid of a hand lens, you might study the delicious intricacy of a snowflake and imagine your way into its microcosmic universe. Each translucent crystal is a tiny world of water molecules ordered into hexagonal crowns. Crowns of thrumming molecules link to other crowns, millions upon millions arrayed in a latticed sheet, arranged like cells in a bee's honeycomb. Sheets stack upon sheets to form an individual snowflake, which itself might contain more than ten billion billion molecules of water.

All forms of snow crystals are some variation on the basic theme of a hexagon, an exterior expression of an internal molecular order, all built from water molecules arranged in interlocked hexagons. A snowflake assembles itself within a cloud as molecules of water condense from vapor, perhaps around a grain of pollen or a speck of dust. From this tiny seed of ice, the crystal grows as more water molecules come twirling out of the air and dock onto its emergent form—a hexagonal prism, shaped like a thin cross section cut from a microscopic wooden pencil. Currents of cold air buffet the young snow crystal, sending it swirling about the cloud through regions with varying temperature and humidity.

Both conditions affect the rates at which water molecules vibrate out of the cloud and lock into the framework of the growing snow crystal—and where on the crystal's faces they will tend to do so. In parts of the cloud where humidity is high, water molecules gravitate toward the snow crystal's protruding corners, causing the snowflake to sprout branchlets. It takes on the feathery, fernlike form we most commonly imagine when we think of snowflakes, the same form a child might cut lovingly from paper, as I did so often when I was a young, dreamy kid, wishing for snow I would not see in earnest until I was in college. By contrast, in particularly cold parts of the cloud with low humidity, the snowflake grows more evenly and crystallizes into a hexagonal plate. As the snowflake voyages through the great body of a cloud, the particulars of its crystalline form will vary from its core to its rim, retaining a record of its travels from the moment of its emergence to the moment that it tumbles out of the cloud and falls toward earth. The snowflake's form holds a story of wandering.

~ ~ ~

A single crystal of snow is fragile and delicate. But consider the strength that lies in numbers. In the obscuring flurry of a Sierra winter storm, the mountains go pale, become a monochrome of gray and white, or disappear altogether. Snow blasts for hours, sometimes days, denuding conifer branches of needles, abrading silvery bark from thin saplings. Snow gathers in crooks of tree limbs, clings to pine and fir needles. Twigs heap among mounds of accumulating snow. Branches yield and bend toward ground. A few great old limbs give way in thundering cracks, landing with booming *wooooofs*. Some trees yield completely, especially young, limber-limbed mountain hemlocks, who bend in prostration beneath the weight of snow.

In the Sierra's high mountain passes, jets of wind blast exposed boles of the range's high-dwelling pine species—lodgepole, whitebark, foxtail. Wind-driven snow abrades trees clean down to the gold of heartwood. Trees are bannered by the passing of countless winter storms, which strip western, storm-fronting faces of trunks bare of branches. Leeward limbs, protected in the storm-sheltered wind shadows, point the way for storms to come.

When at last a winter storm breaks in the Sierra, it catches its breath, sighs, and yawns. It packs its bags, moves on to the east to rail against sky-island forests of the Great Basin. The next morning, an azure sky reveals a blanket of accumulated snow perhaps a meter thick. When evening comes with a slim-mooned sky, you might see the mountains bathed in an amethyst light. Soon bright constellations turn overhead, the snow luminescing as though lit from within.

Come late spring, the sun returns to climb the sky and melt it all, each memory of storm evanescing. Meltwater trickles down through a mosaicked slush of ice crystals in the snowpack to what waits beneath: seeds; the fine-haired roots of storm-battered trees; wispy filaments of fungal mycelia hidden in dark soil. Where snow has accumulated against bare rock, meltwater coalesces to tendrils and rivulets over the bedrock's back, trickles into fissures, enters the subterranean labyrinth of the mountains' fractured body. It journeys through an underworld but it will find its way back, returning to the light by seeps and springs, blooming to rivers who sing down the deep evergreen canyons of the Sierra Nevada.

—RJN

When I was a young high school student, ungainly, pimply, and dumb as a post, I remember the first time I looked through a microscope. In focus was some pale, rather dirty, somewhat malodourous pond water. I was stunned at the color and minute variety of creatures that came into view: they raced, waited, darted, made hairpin turns, showed off svelte figures and profiles so sleek and streamlined that sharks everywhere should be jealous. They had bodies of a most considered and intricate precision of organization; like arabesques.

It shook me out of my teenage stupor. The dead mass of my brain tissue began to show a few tiny, winking lights. Not many years later, someone told me the story of Wilson Bentley, a Vermont farmer who, unlike his neighbors, decided in 1885 that he would try to photograph a snowflake. At age nineteen, after four years of absolute, crashing failure, he did it. He would stand outside in the cold for hours on end, waiting to catch a snowflake . . . with a feather, or a little blackboard. Then he'd place it gingerly under the camera lens, which he had connected to his microscope.

He had hit his stride. He carried on for the next forty-one years, heaven keep him and bless him. All told, he delivered to the world over five thousand miraculous and exact images of snowflakes. He stated that no two are alike.

As a young man, I ordered Bentley's book and remembered the pond water. The world around us is not what we see. It holds a life-giving, gift-giving, invisible order everywhere and always. It is an order of musical and exultant beauty. It has a mysterious and radiant splendor. Everywhere we look, if we would look, the natural world is making beauty, without fanfare, and the work is so plain, intelligent, playful, and devoted, that there is only one word for it: cosmic.

Many years later, I learned that the astronomers working with the Hubble telescope were curious about a patch of deep space that seemed to hold very few stars—a dim and dull patch. So they focused the telescope there and took one of the first photographs of deep space, looking at the universe as it was thirteen billion years ago.

The photo, called the Hubble Ultra Deep Field, is now famous worldwide: it shows us in that dark patch a wilderness of galaxies so numerous and gorgeous that it looks like a field of wildflowers, a rapture of jewels and gold; it is darkness turned to infinite possibility and promise.

Pond water, deep space, snowflakes . . . is there any miracle not offered us?

After moving slowly and gingerly up through a snowfield, we looked back from the pass at the long curve of our tracks in the snow, tiny like the marks of birds. I freed myself of the crampons, and had these questions:

Does deep space notice the erotic curves
Of the snowdrifts?

Do the big pines lean down in amazement
And admiration?

How can snowflakes offer us sinuously and easily
Perfection in every detail?

How are they able to unite joyfully
Sharp dry cold and intricate sensuality?

Snow crystals in sunlight—how do they
Wink in so many colors at once?

Are they teaching us about the play, timing,
And natural internal order of light?

The natural order of the mind?

When a single snow crystal flashes in the air,
Does a distant galaxy tilt toward us?

Do the wildflower seeds in soil love
Their thick white soft blanket?

Do they feel recognized and protected?

Do they need that loving protection to mix
In secret their iridescent colors?

Do they understand how the snow
Holds the water they need?

And snow and sunlight and wildflowers,
Have they always been in cahoots?

Does snow say: I offer all my crystals
And with sunlight I will make clarity?

And does sunlight say: to the clarity
We make, I will add radiance?

And then the wildflowers say: with clarity
And radiance, I will make soft joy?

—SN

GLACIER

A man who keeps company with glaciers comes to feel tolerably insignificant by and by.

—Mark Twain

Oh, science, with your tricks and alchemies,
chain the glacier with sun and wind and tide,
rebuild the gates of ice . . .

—Gillian Clarke

8/7/17, Day 5. Moraine Lake. Woke up early to walk down to the water and watch the sunrise over Moraine Lake and the cold sky bloom from indigo to pale dawn as stars faded. Everyone else still sleeping. Quiet but for the hush of wind in the pine needles and the lapping of the lake. A surround of beautiful old foxtails and lodgepoles. Deb joined me and we watched the blue shadows on some unnamed massive cirque in the distance. Chickadees singing hey sweetie in the lodgepole branches. We all bathed in the lake, got a good cold soaking before our descent into Kern Canyon. It's going to be a hot one.

Wandering a patch of meadow in the high country, you may come upon a curving shape of bent grass where a deer has lain. The deer's twinned toeprints lead to the banks of a meltwater stream. Your mind wanders beneath the water's surface, over the flickering amber of stream gravel to the pawed, spongy earth on the opposite bank and to the tawny meadow beyond. You imagine the deer foraging among grasses and wildflowers. You see how this place holds the deer, how the land has a memory, how you might read the traces of what has come before.

Far in the distance, scrims of ice cleave like old candlewax to the sawtoothed Sierra. The range's crest sweeps down to fluting cradles that once held the bodies of glaciers. You see how the stone once held ice. Late snow clings to the granite in a memory, but it won't last the summer.

Photographs of glaciers often depict them as ethereal things, looming above a great frozen terrain or angling down some austere summit of rock. In such images, the glacier is a body at rest, perhaps at peace. Cobalt veins of ice marble its translucent body. Pale skylight sifts through centuries of its crystalline layers. The glaciers of these photographs are rarefied, pristine, permanent. Such glaciers are objects of desire, images of longing. Roam about a real glacier and look closely, carefully. Lay your hands on its cold, massive, living bulk. Its interior is gorged with stone and grit, its surface gray with dust. Glaciers are messy and burdened. They ruminate and mumble. They are broken. They are losing themselves.

Consider a serac. A serac is a house-sized column of glacial ice. It is a massive glacial splinter bounded by crevasses—the deep, azure cracks that rive a glacier's skin. To get the idea of a serac, score a halved avocado with crisscrossing slices without penetrating all the way to the skin. Bend the avocado from below, gently stretching its surface. Little avocado seracs, separated by knife-drawn crevasses, split away from each other. Real seracs are enormous. Unstable. They loom above, leaning in. They could topple over at any moment, sealing you in a tomb of ice.

Seracs reveal a glacier's insides. Ice within a glacier is stratified, a record of annual snowfall, each layer a page in a diary of storms. Like all mountain glaciers, those of the Sierra began high up in the range where massing snow persisted in shadowed mountain cradles through summer. Accumulating masses of snow gradually thickened and compressed layers lower down into translucent, crystalline ice. Though glaciers have expanded across and retreated from the range numerous times during the past two-and-a-half million years, the glaciers now in the Sierra emerged only a few centuries ago when California's climate turned cooler and wetter for several hundred years, many millennia after the passage of the last great ice age. Ice accumulated layer after layer, year after year, collecting traces of dust born of volcanic eruptions, of forest pollen and forest fires, of the industrial revolution, of nuclear explosions. Bubbles dispersed throughout the glaciers' mosaics of crystalline ice preserved tiny time capsules of trapped air, bearing witness to the increasing concentration of greenhouse gases in the atmosphere. Bubbles compressed as ice thickened, the ice attaining a mass so great it slowly collapsed under its weight, yielding to gravity in a slow, fluid cascade downslope.

Look past the layers of hazy, translucent ice and you'll see a glacier carries remains of mountains. Glacial ice holds mammoth-sized stones, stones the size of abandoned vehicles, stones the size of torsos, the dismembered, broken wreckage of mountains. Much of this burden consists of crushed, nearly obliterated, speck-sized remains of rock ground to a powder as fine as confectioner's sugar— what geologists like to call rock flour. This powdered rock disgorges into the cold, steel-colored meltwater that bleeds from a glacier's disintegrating snout. Meltwater gathers into braided, roiling, muddy watercourses, transforming downstream into jade and turquoise veins.

Retreating glaciers discharge their burdens of stone in chaotic heaps called moraine. Following a glacier's tracks in the Sierra, you must cross sprawling wastelands of moraine if you are to ascend to what might remain of the glacier's frozen body. Bear-sized boulders seesaw as you step and leap among them. The giant stones grind and gnash in protest until the air smells of broken rock. As you ascend, you will happen upon smooth, curving, moraine-free pavements. They are intact parts of the mountain. Parallel grooves inscribe the pavements, tracing the paths of pebbles embedded in the glacier's sliding belly. In places, the ice-honed rock is brilliant and shimmering, as though wet with sheens of water, for all about you water drips and rings in silver threads. But it is the rock itself, polished to a mirror-smooth finish by ice-borne rock flour, that flashes so brightly in the sun. Look farther upslope, beyond the moraine, where what is left of a glacier remains—a scab of gray, layered ice clinging to the blade of the mountain's precipice.

Flying high over the Sierra, it appears as though someone has been at work with an enormous gouge, excavating scoops of stone from the mountain. But it was ice, of course, that did this work: freezing itself into fissures, plucking out rock until it hollowed out and filled stadium-sized amphitheaters, leaving only a few sinuous ridges of vertebral mountain exposed above the sprawling glacier. Downslope from the ice-bitten terrain, moraine lies in sheets that limn the curving traces of long-disappeared, tonguing muscles of ice. The ice sprawled from icefields the size of metropolises and plunged down ice-sculpted valleys, the selfsame valleys that today hold the tributaries of the Sierra's great rivers and that cradle its forests, flower gardens, and dreaming deer. We see by signs where the glaciers have lain and where they have wandered. In a century, decades perhaps, the land will know glaciers only as a memory.

—RJN

The anthropologist and cognitive scientist Gregory Bateson once made a provocative and brilliant proposition about the mind. He observed that the conscious mind must attend and respond to the myriad daily changes in the world, as we make our way through the thicket of events that comprise our days. We receive, however, through our senses, a far greater quantity of material than that small portion of which we are conscious. And what do our minds make of this material? How does it hold and use what is received?

Bateson's answer was this: that which resides in our unconscious is the permanently true: our constant, sustaining, trustworthy relation to the earth, a beautiful unity with the world that sustains our daily life. We must do the obvious and carry this concept to its natural conclusion: the earth lives in us, and we live within the earth. Our unconscious is the light and air and water and soil of the mind, all at work in service of life. This means, among many other things, that Freud was not merely wrong, he was exactly and disastrously wrong: rather than a den of suppressed conflicts, memories, and turmoil, the unconscious mind is a workaday and beautiful connection to reality that shapes and enriches us. Learning the depth and extent of such connection can be daunting or even terrifying, but it can lead us onward to healing and wholeness.

Which brings me to glaciers: perhaps the slow, invisible work of these massive forms, in service of life and creation, mirrors the hidden work of the mind. The labor is continuous, formative, and full of matter. Mountains are carved and marked, great monoliths of rock are cracked and transported, canyons and fjords are created, valleys are opened in preparation for rivers, the fine dust of experience is collected. Yet as we walk in the high mountains, we cannot perceive immediately this work. It is slow, patient, and concealed. It reveals itself to us only in time, as we work and sketch, read and look and learn; until slowly, in the Sierra, we can see the grand and world-making effects of such labors.

In a similar way, as we do our work in the world, as we write and love, learn and reflect, there are times when the unconscious is made conscious, and we can lose ourselves in wonder and astonishment at our luck of having with earth so ebullient a unity. At such fortunate times, we vanish into the world and come into a visceral sense of the abiding and abundant intelligence all around us. And this sense, often, is strengthened in love and by dreams, for dreams are the equivalent to the seracs of glaciers: we see inside the mind, in all its natural powers of play and creation. We see the hidden work that shapes and sustains us.

It is as if we can enter the world of the poet William Blake:

> "If the doors of perception were cleansed, everything would appear . . . as it is, infinite."

> "To the eyes of a man of imagination, nature is imagination itself."

> "Man has no Body distinct from his soul; for that called Body is a portion of a Soul discerned by the five senses, the chief inlets of Soul in this age."

> "If a thing loves, it is infinite."

We might almost say that, once our sight turns to vision by means of understanding, we learn that the mind is not made of nature, but rather nature is made of mind. We are enveloped, by sudden deliverance, in the rich, generous, gift-giving, deep order of the natural world.

And look at what is made: from the labors of the cold, sonorous, hidden, enormous, mountain-grinding glaciers, one summer day in the Sierra we walk in the middle of a soft green meadow with a clear stream full of dragonflies, and all around us resurgent, longed-for, soft, lustrous wildflowers, and above us the ridges of rock polished by the glacier that gave form to the valley where we stand. In the distance, tawny deer stand in the sunlight.

> Where granite ridges stand high—sails
> To catch the wind of universal gales,
>
> So that this earth may turn; where
> Wildflowers are tempest and delectation,
> Soft minute heavenly testimony; where
>
> Lakes watch the clouds, sun, stars,
> Moon—then, brushed by the wind,
> Show a light within; where the tars,
> Quicksand, mistake, shame, chagrin,
>
> Hatred and death-cult in our history
> Are set aside forever, all degradation
> Is undone, we see our plain story:
>
> Soul is made of water, rock, and sky.
> Like them we live, like them we die.

—SN

RIVER

Nations die
rivers go on
mountains
go on

—Japanese Proverb

Let your attention to the beauty of the running stream
Lead you to the sweetness of the rain from Heaven.

—Jalaludin Rumi

. . . the dancing river, the dancing blood, the dancing grass, the whole
revolving world.

—Jean Giono

The mountains rise up, but wither they must
And the rivers will lose their wanderlust
Leaves of gold turn to rust
And what will become of us, we are beautiful dust.

—Deborah Levoy

8/7/17, Day 5. Kern Canyon. Rough time coming down into the canyon. My day to bonk. Something about the heat coming off the rocks. Grumpy and edgy and hot all the way down. Lightheaded. Nervous about snakes. Stay vigilant. Pay attention. When we finally make it to the river, I'm done. I pull off my boots and fall fully clothed into the water, cram technicolor jellybeans into my mouth, say nothing for at least twenty minutes, and just breathe at the surface, submersed like a frog.

The Sierra Nevada is an immense, curving spine of rock winding four hundred miles down the length of California. A profile cut across the range reveals a ramp. It eases up from California's central valley to the mountains' frost-riven crest, then plummets down a steep escarpment to the sagebrushed scrubland of the Great Basin. Yet such geometric description of the range is only abstraction. For the Sierra Nevada is alive, sheathed in a skin of soil and forests, veined with green canyons holding cold rivers in indigo shadows.

Rivers have sawn down through the mountains, cutting to the quick of the range's granitic interior, drawing the mountains down in an unending litany of clattering cobbles, tumbling sand, gritty silt, and dust. Rivers have ferried all matter of fragmented stone to the yawning central valley, on to the muddy bay of San Francisco, and into the dark, dreaming chasm of the Pacific Ocean.

The names of the Sierra's great rivers—Feather, Yuba, American, Cosumnes, Mokelumne, Stanislaus, Tuolumne, Merced, San Joaquin, Kings, Kaweah, Kern, and Tule, which roam the range's forested western slope; and the Truckee, Carson, Walker, and Owens of the Sierra's arid, rain-shadowed east—bear the imprint of tongues of those who knew and traveled the land: Native, Spanish, Anglo. Some names are familiar, knowable, but other names have been lost, obscured, erased from cultural memory, or perhaps remembered by only a few.

Before California was California, some one hundred million years ago, the primeval forebearer of the Pacific Ocean lapped against what is today the Sierra Nevada's western edge. Into this shallow sea, ancestral rivers unloaded their hauls of Sierran rock in such quantity that the seafloor sagged and sank under the accumulating weight. Remnants of the river-ferried and ocean-sifted sediments are stacked between the Sierra and the Coast Ranges in a bulging wedge of rock up to six miles thick. The volume of it might fill the Grand Canyon twenty-five times over. Yet still this mass says nothing of the Sierra's remains that were gorged out by rivers, dumped into the ancestral Pacific, and then dragged down into the earth's incandescent interior along the conveyer belt of subduction, the engine that drives the slow process of tectonic churning by which the planet consumes its rocky skin, regenerates the contours of its surface, closes and opens its ocean basins, and draws its landmasses together to build continents only to divide them later from within. Which is to say that most of the Sierra has gone down the river.

Layered rock outcrops bearing scraps of the Sierra's river-borne past poke out from the grassy, oak-dotted hillsides of the western edge of California's sunburnt central valley. Each tilted layer is a page of sediment laid down at the sea-soaked feet of the Sierra's ancient river deltas or jumbled farther offshore by undersea avalanches. The leaves of maritime stone are inscribed with eroded grit drawn from Sierra-topping volcanoes, now long gone, and the cauldrons that supplied them with molten rock from below. All of these remains were carried by rivers.

Hidden among the pages of stone like forgotten notes are layers of chert, a rock made from billions of skeletons of radiolaria, microscopic sea-dwelling organisms who, with their improvisational and kaleidoscopic forms, drifted through the Mesozoic ocean as though in a hallucinogenic fever-dream.

Travel east across the central valley, up into the Sierra's dusty, ponderosa-flocked foothills, and you surge fifty million years forward in time to bona-fide river deposits now exposed in highway roadcuts. The stream-bottom remains—pitched hundreds, sometimes thousands of feet above the courses of the Sierra's modern rivers—lie about in thick, rusty piles of cobbles hiding nubs and flecks of gold, all cemented and bound together by grit and time.

The ancient gold-ferrying rivers traveled west down a broad welt of mountains hundreds of miles wider than the present-day Sierra. That welt of rock rose in what is now eastern Nevada and tilted down to a shallow, lagoon-necklaced sea just west of the modern boundary of the Sierra foothills. Rivers wandered the fat range through evergreen subtropical forests of magnolia, breadfruit, fig, palm, persimmon, and laurel—the trees twined with moonseed vines. All this lush vegetation rooted itself down in soils weathered a deep brick red in the balmy and humid climate of a younger Sierra. Today you can still find remnants of these old red soils exposed along roadcuts lower down in the Sierra's western flank. And you can still trace the paths of a few of the ancestral rivers, preserved where steaming lava flows poured into their valleys like molten metal into casts.

It is said that Heraclitus of Ephesus, a philosopher of Ancient Greece, once stated that we cannot step into the same river twice. Consider the North Fork of the Yuba, in the Sierra's north. Its jade waters glide through a vertiginous green canyon cut into the stone of ancient oceanic islands. The islands drifted into the western edge of North America, assembling California in a parade of tectonic collisions as scrims of a shimmery, silver-green rock called serpentinite, metamorphosed from slivers of Earth's mantle, slithered up between them. Cobbles of this ancient stone lie strewn about the river's bottom, glinting like reptilian eyes. Watch from the river's edge and you might see a snake gliding out over the water's surface. The snake divides the water, ringing out ripples of green and silver across this river of ten thousand voices.

Or consider the Tuolumne, in the heart of the range. On its banks of one-hundred-million-year-old granite, honed smooth by glaciers and the tumbling of river stones, you might cup its water in your hands, gather the light of clouds, and let its cold, liquid body spill over your skin. Luminous wildflowers sway in the surrounding meadow, moving in time with the river's insistent rhythm. The streamside flowers will wither to husks, their seeds will wait in the ground, and stones will keep rolling on down their river.

Or consider the Marble Fork of the Kaweah, in the Sierra's south. There is a place along the Kaweah's course where its current spills through a great bear of a boulder halved like an apple. Just downstream, the current divides around a smooth slab of granite that will hold you as if it were the palm of God. Step out across half submerged stones to reach this sacred place, sit down with a child you love, hold her in your arms, keep her warm against the chill morning air. As beams of sun split through branches of pine and fir. As a water ouzel dances beneath the current. As a song sparrow sings from the willow branches on the bank. As granite cobbles whirl in pot holes, round over centuries to small moons. Hold your child close, for when you return, the river will have moved on, and she will be a woman.

—RJN

We began our hike knowing that it had been a big winter and that the massive snow drifts in the mountains had turned rivulets into rocketing creeks and rivers into threatening torrents. Before we began hiking, we knew that already three hikers had drowned in the Kern.

Our route had many watercourses that we had meant to walk across. Now, a coursing and tossing of fresh currents confronted us at every crossing, and we had to reconnoiter up-canyon and down-canyon to find a way forward that would not kill us. It carried the terror of knowing the precise number of mistakes allowed: one, and one only.

My balance is poor. More than once, I crawled slowly like a clumsy lizard over tree trunks. Our daughters, though, leapt up easily upon the same trunks and walked straight across with insouciance and exquisite balance, for all the world as if out for a Sunday promenade.

The combination was unforgettable: unbearable beauty and the presence of death. Emily Dickinson wrote, "Those that are worthy of life are of miracle, for life is a miracle, and death, harmless as a bee, except to those who run."

We did not run. We tried to learn. What stayed with us was the power of water, and its movement, which is irresistible, mountain-making, and on the move with the force of revelation. As a river is to a mountain, so is our gathered experience to our years on earth. As rivers shape the material of the Sierra, so does the arcing and concentrated movement of our ideas, actions, and spirit shape our days and months. It is as if a river is a teacher, coming in tumult, with flashing and threaded currents, the cream of white water, deep earthly music, and the hypnotically graceful, rhythmic curving descent toward the sea. And what it teaches is to follow a course forward based on a river's ancient recommendations: a suppleness of mind, a communion with land, a certainty of joy, an openness to light, and a surety of destination. When we are alongside a river for any spell of time, a thankfulness wells up abundantly within us. Each river is a convocation of astonishments. We want to bring them close, and understand them, learning from them the phosphorescent style of their ancient, present, cut-loose liberty of work in the world. Moving along the trail, I wanted to share every wild river's comely beauties and uncanny instruction.

> A river—healer,
> Acrobat, musician, traveler—
> Going home.

> A river—at work,
> Our weaver, daily trusted
> Artisan of light.

> A river—sidekick,
> Professor of flashing,
> Skylarking child.

> A river—on the move,
> Conjuring-book of clouds,
> Pathway made of sky.

> A river—who
> Needs to rest, once
> Having heaven's rhythm?

> A river—light
> And clarity in love
> Again. And again.

> A river—open
> Simple, normal, plain, common
> Transcendental whirling.

> A river—going
> Through gates of paradise
> Every second.

A river—our
Strange honeycomb of light,
    Traveling laughter.

A river—falling,
Rising, all jets, geysers,
    Canters, backflips.

A river—cascade
Of angel feathers, soil,
    Mayflies, willow-leaves.

A river—meeting ground
Of whirlpools, dragonflies,
    Ebullience, peace.

A river—showing,
On whitewater, black shadow
    Of the passing eagle.

A river—gambol,
Somersault, cavort, skip, cartwheel,
    Then meditative eddy.

—SN

FOREST

As the world warms, the sea rises, the forest burns, and our fellow-creatures suffer, there will still be beauty. Beauty to take comfort in. Beauty to mourn.

—Max Norman

8/8/17, Day 6. Kern Hot Springs. Last night we dipped in the hot springs, which are too hot, you have to add cold water from the river. Full moon last night. We made a fire, conversation subdued. The sun doesn't fully begin to enter the canyon until 9 a.m. A Douglas squirrel dive bombed our tent near dawn. Its chatter and that of several of its relatives the only sounds I could make out above the Kern's roar. In this canyon no sound but the raging of the Kern. Have to be close to each other in order to understand one another.

Each spring, the sun climbs, the snows of winter thaw, and the Sierra Nevada again inhales life into its montane forests. Deer draw up from the sere western Sierra foothills and the stark eastern escarpment. Black bears emerge from hibernal dens. Butterflies, some of whom have waited out winter ensconced in narrow crevices of bark, take to the wing. Migrating birds arrive from near and far to feast on a bounty of insects and berries and to build their nests among conifer branches. Lupines and asters and paintbrushes bloom at forests' sunlit edges as young of every kind take their first steps and try their wings.

There has not always been a spring emergence in the Sierra's forests, of course, for the range has not always been forested. Forests are migrants too. Great rivers of ice once roamed where today the dark sylvan fur of conifers burrs the landscape. As glaciers retreated, species of pine and cedar and fir and hemlocks marched their way up into the high country, trailing the hems of melting glaciers. The advancing conifers shed tiny seeds, carried by wind and animals to find good grounding among the fine, nutritious detritus of glacial moraine. Forests offered abiding animal orchardists prospect and protection, sustenance and home.

The annual rhythm of the Sierra's inhalation and exhalation of life, drawing animals up and into the mountains in spring and then exhaling them down and out in autumn, mirrors the movement of a much slower rhythm of migration that has breathed glaciers and forests in and out of the great granitic spine of the Sierra Nevada for the last two-and-a-half million years. Eleven thousand years ago, at the end of Earth's most recent glaciation, glaciers sprawled across the range like sleeping cats. Forests grew at the Sierra's edges, at much lower elevations than they do today. Giant sequoias flourished at the range's western boundary with California's Central Valley as well as near the shores of a then much deeper and more expansive Mono Lake, located at the foot of the Sierra's eastern edge, the surrounds of which are now a sagebrush desert. Only about 4,500 years ago did giant sequoias migrate to their present neighborhoods of eighty or so groves in the western Sierra. It's possible that some of the oldest sequoia monarchs now standing in the Sierra are members of only the second generation to have ever lived there. It's more likely that giant sequoias have moved in and out of the mid elevations of the range dozens of times, as glaciers have advanced, then retreated, again and again. Whatever the case, however primeval the Sierra's forests might appear, this semblance of ancientness is an artifact of a limited temporal perception. Forests move.

The migration of forests up and down the Sierra is a slow dance, synchronized with rhythmic cycles in the eccentricity of Earth's orbit and the tilt and wobble of the Earth's rotational axis. These orbital gyrations, pulsing over periods of tens of thousands of years, vary the intensity of sunlight striking Earth over time. Changes in the intensity of sunlight in high northern latitudes is key, it turns out, to regulating glacial cycles—and thus to the distribution of forest. This is in part because the concentration of continental landmass around the north pole offers ample runway for glaciers (and forests) to advance or retreat. Furthermore, ice cover in the high northern latitudes affects the global cycling of carbon, which in turn regulates the concentration of atmospheric carbon dioxide that acts as a planetary thermostat. This thermostat ultimately helps regulate glacial growth and retreat in relatively low latitude, high elevation regions like the Sierra Nevada. The upshot is that Earth's orbital variations drive a causal chain that governs the distribution of glaciers, and therefore forests, in the Sierra.

~ ~ ~

Other changes in the Sierra's forest occur much faster. Recent warming in the range, brought on by increasing average global temperature caused by greenhouse gas emissions from human activities, has pushed seedlings of several of the range's iconic conifer species—the mountain hemlock, the red fir, the western white pine—to start putting down roots at elevations more than a hundred meters higher than where they did a century ago.

And now the Sierra forest is transforming on a time scale we can see. In 2015, when California was in the midst of a brutal, six-year drought, trees of the lower elevations of the Sierra Nevada—incense cedar and several species of pine, fir, and oak—were beginning to die en masse, particularly in the range's warmer southern regions. By 2016, many old sequoia giants in groves near our trailhead had begun to shed foliage high up in their canopies, hundreds of feet above ground, in an apparent attempt to cope with ongoing water stress. Today, not far from our trailhead, you can now look out across undulating ribs of mountains and see for miles and miles that much of the once dark sea of conifer forest is dead. Tree after tree is the color of burnt orange, the needles as brittle as rust, marked for the conflagration that will inevitably come. As of this writing in 2020, more than 147 million trees have perished in the Sierra Nevada as the result of the drought, whose effects persist despite the record amount of snow accumulation during the spectacular winter preceding our range-crossing journey in 2017. The snow simply came too late for the trees.

There is a deep ache in looking out on endless miles of dead conifer trees—on seeing an entire landscape of once green, singing forest silenced by drought. Part of the self withers inside in the presence of death at such a scale. The scene is . . . apocalyptic.

I try to remember that the land is older than I can know. Every tree, every last one of them, will fall and return to earth. The forests of the Sierra, like all things, must change. I try to remember too that an apocalypse, taken literally, means a revelation of knowledge, an uncovering of truth. The mountains hold their own stories of birth and death, of departure and returning, of joy and of mourning. All is impermanent. The Sierra knows time long before we walked the Earth. It will endure long after we have left it, long after we have made our last footprint in its dust and scratched our last marks on its stone. When I returned to visit the old groves of sequoia monarchs where we began our journey across the mountains, I could not help but look for seedlings. I found them, lithe and green, reaching toward sunlight.

—RJN

Much of our hike along the High Sierra trail was through forest. After hiking in these mountains for years, one begins to understand how each tree has its preferred elevation, habitat, and orientation to the sun. It is almost like the studied placement of musical instruments in a symphony, each in the place where, by some complex musical intuition, over millennia, they find their concord in the composition of mountain life. As we climbed, that composition played all around us: yellow and sugar pines, white fir and incense cedar at lower elevations; then, as the ascent continued, Jeffrey pine and red fir and western juniper; then, at eight thousand feet, aspen, lodgepole and Western white pine, and after another two-thousand-foot climb, whitebark and foxtail pines. Each has its own character and cone, bark and silhouette, and its own notes to play when the wind comes. The trees are all wind instruments, and their leaves and needles, taken together in their orchestral offerings, are a stagecraft of flashing.

What was it like for us, day after day, as visitors and students, to walk through this beckoning and complex homeland for lilting birds, animate shadows, bats and sinuous rivulets, small meadows, paintbrush and lupine and black bear, columbine and monkey flower, and the cumulative and beautiful mystery, as we walked, of the enveloping and perfected forest? We remembered the observation of John Muir that the clearest way into the universe is through a forest wilderness.

Or as Emily Dickinson put it, "When much in the woods as a little girl, I was told that the snake would bite me, that I might pick a poisonous flower, or goblins kidnap me, but I went along and met no one but angels." Dickinson said also, in an iconic sentence that illuminates all her verse, "I was thinking today—as I noticed, that the 'Supernatural' was only the natural, disclosed."

What is gut-wrenching and heart-piercing is what we have done as a species, with our ignorant and thankless interference: the stopping of fires, the planting of fish, the slow violent contamination of the atmosphere with carbon dioxide; clear-cuts, uncontrolled grazing, the idolatry of exploitation rather than the life-giving labor of understanding.

Yet we were able to have nearly two weeks walking in a forest that has come round to its present magnificence after tens of millions of years of the most dramatic transformations: baked by heat that blazed in epochs when there were rain forests at the earth's poles, and crushed by a tonnage of ice in the glacial periods.

There is nothing more powerful than the movement toward beauty. As we walked, this thought sustained us. What we needed was to keep moving: one more day, and in each day, all day, one more step. It struck me as the simplest rule of life and of reflection: keep moving. Stay in readiness. Cultivate openness, clarity, affection, an easygoing revelry of the senses, a trust in our luck that we are here on earth at all, that we have this moment at all. Movement along a trail is movement within the mind. In the long run, the revelation of beauty is not a matter of chance: it is the centermost surety in life. The forest is in league with our dreams.

> One more step—
> Poisoned arrow
>   Just missed you.

> One more step—
> Wisp of light
>   At root of mind.

> One more step—
> Into the eye
>   Of cyclonic beauty.

> One more step—
> Shows the soul the way
>   To mind's allspice.

> One more step—
> The day a hinge
>   Between worlds.

One more step—
Liberty in you like
    Eagles, oceans.

One more step—
Radiant dream stands up
    And gets real.

One more step—
Your headband is
    The Milky Way.

One more step—
You see how miracle
    Wears raggedy clothes.

One more step—
Daughters take wing
    Fly around the sky.

One more step—
A friend whose hands
    Harvest light.

One more step—
Lightning leaves a note
    In your hand.

One more step—
Questions with no answers
    Except you.

One more step—
Dreams mix colors
    You paint with.

One more step—
A future century
    Finds you ready.

One more step—
You sowing seeds
    Of another cosmos.

One more step—
You reach into your pocket
   Find there Reality.

One more step—
After six decades
   You stop bleeding.

One more step—
You know the language
   Of owls.

One more step—
Even a fingernail
   Has prodigious magic.

One more step—
You can heal anyone
   And no one knows.

One more step—
Everything you see, a gift
   Bristling with infinity.

One more step—
Uncanny spark that can
   Kindle a mind.

One more step—
Trail turns into
   A tempest of promise.

                                        —SN

FIRE

My fingers emit sparks of fire with Expectation of my future labors.

—William Blake

The seeker after truth is a traveler who purifies himself like fire from smoke.

—Shabistari

8/8/17, Day 6, PM. Arrived Junction Meadow. Day of sketchy stream crossings across Rock Creek, Whitney Creek, Wallace Creek, and so many others I lost count. It took us almost an hour to find a safe passage over Whitney, but the girls bounded across the logs like ballerina squirrels. Water pouring into this canyon after the big snow year. I am tired. Steve is losing feeling in one of his legs. Lucy impervious to all suffering as is G apparently; she is floating across these mountains as if made of clouds. Hoping for an easier day tomorrow, even though we're climbing out of the canyon. Quiet magical evening beneath the moon shadows of the old trees.

Wherever you might wander in a Sierra forest, evidence of its primeval relationship with fire is close at hand. Dig through the conifer-needled duff of a forest floor. Expose fists of cracked granite bound with ropy tree roots, and you'll spot flecks of blue-black charcoal glinting among fragments of soil and stone, holding memories of embers. Probe the layers of fine silt at the bottom of a forest-nestled lake, and you'll come upon tiny fragments of charred wood—the remnants of fire's frequent visits to the surrounding watershed over thousands of years.

Or look at the trees themselves. The trees have learned, evolutionarily speaking, not just to reckon with fire, but to rely on it. In the dry oak savannahs of the range's foothills, the rangy, splayed branches of the gray pine, the Sierra's lowest growing conifer, are studded with massive, bract-clawed cones as big as pineapples. For years, I wondered why this hardy tree would invest so much effort into producing woody fruits of such astonishingly preposterous heft and size, until it dawned on me that this was an investment in the future—an adaptation conferring protection from flame to its interior treasure of thick-hulled seeds.

Venture a few thousand feet higher into the range, into the heart of the Sierra's mid-elevation forests. Look up into the crown of a coniferous Sierra giant: the first branches don't splay out from the trunk for at least a couple of stories. The trees discard their lower limbs as they grow upward, casting off ladder-rungs of branches that might otherwise carry flame into canopies. Examine the tree trunks. Mosaics of thick, umber-hued plates of bark armor the boles of ponderosa and Jeffery pines, defending against the heat of conflagrations. Millennia-old giant sequoias wrap themselves in foot-and-a-half-thick sheaths of fibrous, fire-resistant bark that insulate the tree's sensitive, nutrient-conducting tissues. Even still, many of the old sequoia giants, though still very much alive, have been chimneyed out by flames that burned up into the heartwood.

But giant sequoias also need fire. Fire quite literally prepares the ground for the next generation by clearing the forest floor of accumulated duff and exposing the bare mineral soil that seeds need to germinate. The sequoia produces myriad cones the size of walnuts, which after developing remain sealed for decades until the intense heat of a good fire dries them out, coaxing the cones to let go their tiny, tight-fisted grips and let fall gentle rains of seeds. Fire opens the forest canopy, letting in light that young saplings need to grow. Fire is to the giant sequoia forest what butterflies and bees are to the range's alpine flower gardens—a generous accomplice in the plant's regeneration. In the Sierra, there's always been a give and take between forests and fire. There's always been a co-reliance.

For millennia, lightning-ignited—and eventually Native-tended—fires fed among the Sierra's mid-elevation forests and helped maintain complex, diverse crazy quilts of patchy forest habitat in various stages of fire recovery and forest succession. Indigenous peoples used fire in the Sierra's mid-elevation forests as one tool in a suite of horticultural technologies to tend to the wild—to shape a sylvan universe in which both human and nonhuman kin collaborated in a continuous act of creation and renewal. The natural rhythms of fire, complemented by this time-honored practice of fire gardening, produced a varied mosaic of forest habitat that included lichen-flocked old-growth forests; spindly, fire-ravaged snag forests with carpets of emergent saplings; and open-canopied groves of widely spaced trees, with plenty of room to let in the gentle blue light of the Sierra sky.

This Sierra forest mosaic was a milieu run through with edges, a kind of liminal forest world through which deer and bear and people could easily travel—a world whose inhabitants could maneuver across boundaries to take refuge in one place and forage or hunt in another. It was the kind of forest in which the Sierra's rare great gray owl could hide among shady stands of trees and search adjacent moon-lit meadows for sustenance. It was the kind of forest in which now threatened animals like the black-backed woodpecker, the California spotted owl, and the ferocious Pacific fisher thrived.

Policies of fire suppression enacted in the late nineteenth and early twentieth centuries turned the forests of the Sierra into a colossal, unintentional ecological experiment—a fire exclosure at the scale of a mountain range. Today, many of the Sierra's forested landscapes captured in historical photographs are almost unrecognizable, save for the contours of the mountain peaks in the distance. Where once stood open, parklike expanses dominated by widely spaced ponderosa and Jeffrey pines, now there are continuous, densely vegetated blankets of coniferous green dominated by fire-intolerant white fir and incense cedar. Young trees have massed in the previously open forest gaps, closing canopies and shrouding the ground in shade. In the absence of fire, the once open forest floor has transformed into a jackstraw of fallen branches and boles littering a dry, spongy mantle of brown needles desiccated into a tinderbox. On hot summer days, you can almost smell the piney resin itching to burn. Now, when fire returns from its long exile, it rages.

~ ~ ~

The forests of the Sierra have long endured a liminal existence due to a mismatch in timing between the arrival of precipitation in cooler months and the warm summer growing season—a defining attribute of California's so-called Mediterranean climate. In an average year, the Sierra might intercept a handful of big, wet storms between November and March before the precipitation window closes shut, more or less, for the rest of the year. Given the asynchronous timing between the arrivals of water and warmth, it's a wonder that the Sierra Nevada's forests store among the highest levels of carbon on a per-area basis of any forest in the continental United States. What makes this possible is the Sierra's long growing season, coupled with the fact that the bulk of precipitation has historically reached the range's higher elevations as snow, which slowly releases meltwater deep into summer.

In the past, during relatively normal years, melting snow enabled forest soils to retain enough moisture—with an occasional spritz from a summer shower—to slake trees' thirst through the warm seasonal drought. This remains true as long as fire is allowed to play its venerable role in pruning the Sierra forest, maintaining a relatively open forest structure with trees polka-dotting the landscape rather than cramped together—with a few straws of roots, rather than many, drawing on reserves of water underground. Too little moisture and trees can't marshal flows of sap to defend against onslaughts of bark beetles, which burrow into trees' living flesh and destroy their circulation systems.

As California's climate warms, less snow falls and less snow lingers on through spring to moisten the heart of the range's conifer forests. The forested lands of the Sierra Nevada are warmer, drier, and more fire prone. Fires are burning hotter, lasting longer, consuming larger areas, and even burning more frequently higher up in the range—in the cool, moist, previously fire-resistant lodgepole pine forests—than at any time in recorded history. Some ecologists worry that trees won't recover in the range's mid-elevations once fire and damage by bark-beetles clears them out. They worry that these mid-elevations could be in the midst of a wholesale transition from forest to chaparral. Others think we might be able to work our way back toward a healthy forest mosaic, using prescribed burns that whittle away the backlog of accumulated fuel. One thing is certain though. Fires in the Sierra will only become more devastating and destructive should emissions of planet-warming greenhouse gases continue apace.

~ ~ ~

In 2013, several years before Steven and I traversed the range with our families, I was heading home from an earlier backpacking trip. In the rearview mirror, I saw the reflection of an immense, billowing, gray nimbus. It took me a moment to convince myself that the Sierra hadn't been bombed. As vaporizing forest roiled into the sky, a nightmare of fleeing animals burned across the screen of my mind's eye. The fire raged, raining ash, turning the sky the color of blood. Months later, it finally smoldered out with the first good autumn rain. I traveled that winter to witness the devastation close up. Charred pillars of trees stretched to the horizon. It was a necropolis, a blackened wasteland bitter with the smell of smoke.

I've gone back each year to witness how the forest might recover from such devastation. Seven summers later, the blackened pillars of trees are still very much there, but they stand above a brushy tangle of green. Ferns and tough-leaved native shrubs have sprung up everywhere. Ponderosa pines I thought were surely dead are flush with new brushes of needles. Oaks are regenerating. Tiny conifer seedlings poke through soil glittered with charcoal. Black-backed woodpeckers, their feathers so dark the birds disappear against burn-blackened snags, hammer deep into trunks as they probe for wood-boring beetles. The air is a hum of insects. At day's end, the silhouettes of bats swirl in the gloaming. As the sky darkens, small mammals scurry out from burrows dug beneath downed boles. Some fall prey before the silent flights of owls.

Perhaps in a few decades areas this burned-out landscape will begin to look something like what we think of when think of a forest. But even now this place, this fire forest, this land of blackened snags is a land of wild abundance. Forests and fire have always been companions in the Sierra. May we learn to dance with them again.

—RJN

To some phenomena of nature, we have a reaction that might be called primeval. Bats, rattlesnakes, insect larvae . . . and forest fires. It is as if a raw, ready part of the mind is touched, the scope of our mind is wrenched and pressured by fear, and we are helplessly unable to detach and keep curiosity alive; to try to see the fire whole or to assess the meaning and teaching of what envelops us. Anyone who has confronted the inferno of a furiously advancing forest fire will recall the terror before such power, and the incredulity that anything living could survive.

Yet in the Sierra Nevada, as Richard writes here, fire was and is a life-giving and necessary part of the health of the forest. It is as if the mountains and the forest were in league with the sky, and they made a plan to recognize the excellence and usefulness of thunderbolts. The lightning-led fires in the Sierra created a forest of verdant and magnificent variation: trees old and young, rich nurturing shade alongside meadows of sensuous green, trunks that soar not far from seedlings, vaulted spaces of coolness and colorful lichen, sunlit snags. It is, like so much of the natural history of the range, a teaching story. It is about the way destruction might be a necessary illumination—the way the world marks the beginning of new, lustrous possibilities in life.

Who among us has not been incinerated by a firestorm of events? It could be a scorching childhood, an illness that leaves us laced with pain, a lost love that holds a blowtorch to the heart. Some of us lose parents or loved ones to violence or rampaging illness. All of us must face the virulent cancer of injustice that sickens our times and must watch politics practiced as a consciously enraged and comprehensive hatred.

We suffer. Yet in this legendary mountain range we can learn how colossal ruin can mark the beginning of gentle, patient regeneration; how our dismantling might allow us to remake ourselves; and how incineration may leave us with nothing—nothing, that is, but what counts: what we really need.

Rumi put it this way:

> Truth imposes upon us
> Heat and cold, grief and pain
> Terror and weakness of wealth and body
> Together, so that the coin of our innermost being
> Becomes evident.

I remember times in my life that felt like an end-time: early on, I felt as if I was subject to a years-long lightning strike, with a bolt in the face every day. But slowly I learned, as it were, to look the lightning in the face and be ready. And to use the presence of threat and the imposition of suffering to set off within me a trickery, an antic defiance, a workaday playfulness, so that I might try to find my way to safety, and endeavor there to make a homeland and to recompose a life.

> I can read
> By my own light—
> Incineration.

> This sense of release,
> Who knew—
> Incineration.

> Just the time to hide
> In my shadow—
> Incineration.

> Let's cherish the heat,
> Gather the light—
> Incineration.

Thanks for lighting
My ready torch—
Incineration.

The soul dodges,
Canny dance move—
Incineration.

Thanks for lighting
The candles—
Incineration.

Braiding that fire
Into my brain stem—
Incineration.

The sand of soul
Melted into clarity—
Incineration.

Thank the heavens,
My life was frozen—
Incineration.

To cauterize the gashes
Life must give—
Incineration.

Cooler than my fever,
Flames a relief—
Incineration.

Sometimes, the destruction was so complete, I felt myself to be a compilation of ashes. It brings to mind the Korean proverb: "When the house burns down, save the nails."

Good to be ashes—
Blown high, glittering
With moonlight, sunlight.

Good to be ashes—
Traveling with clouds,
Flashing forward.

Good to be ashes—
In that flashing,
　　A beginning of rhythm.

Good to be ashes—
Scattered, yet
　　Dreams and wings.

Good to be ashes—
A piece of me
　　In the meadow.

Good to be ashes—
A piece of me
　　In the canyon.

Good to be ashes—
A piece of me
　　Riding a river.

Good to be ashes—
A piece of me
　　On a dragonfly's wing.

Good to be ashes—
Made of earth, ready
　　Once more to love.

　　　　　　　　　　　　　　　　　—SN

RANGE OF LIFE

Once in his life a man ought to concentrate his mind upon the remembered earth. He ought to give himself up to a particular landscape in his experience; to look at it from as many angles as he can, to wonder upon it, to dwell upon it. He ought to imagine that he touches it with his hands at every season and listens to the sounds that are made upon it. He ought to imagine the creatures there and all the faintest motions of the wind. He ought to recollect the glare of the moon and the colors of the dawn and dusk.

—Barry Lopez

BIGHORN

Ovis canadensis sierrae

The key to maintaining spiral growth . . . is to allow the outer surface, the surface farthest from the axis around which the coiling takes place, to grow more than the inner surface.

. . . If, at the base of the horn, the leading edge grows more than the trailing edge, the horn curls outward.

—Peter Stevens, *Patterns in Nature*

Why have we ever slandered the outward? The perception of surfaces will always have the effect of miracle to a sane sense.

—Thoreau

The belief that some are superior and some are inferior—whether racism, or sending another species into the oblivion of extinction . . . both grow from the same rotten core.

—J. Drew Lanham

8/9/17, Day 7. Kern Canyon to Crabtree Meadow. Feeling cocky, good in my legs in the cool morning. Told everyone our 2,700-foot climb would be a 'trivial ascent,' a comment which got a raised eyebrow from G. We follow the Kern, turn to follow the canyon up Wallace Creek passing a few fluttering aspens, travel south along the John Muir Trail. Watched as the umber-violet roof pendant atop the Great Western Divide came into view—we were on the other side of the Divide just a few days ago. Musical creek crossings across Wright and Whitney. Magic spells of water. Pack feeling lighter today.

When it comes to the law of gravity, the bighorn is a fugitive, ascending vertical cliffs by way of the narrowest of rock ledges. It is an animal of formidable strength, kinesthetic genius, and most of all, inconceivable fearlessness. To the Sierra bighorn, the blasting of hail in a violent electric storm is but a gentle summer shower. The booms of thunder are but peaceful mountain lullabies. Steep avalanche chutes? They are made for sprinting down, hurtling at full throttle with deft side-to-side leaps to break momentum. Bottomless chasms? They're made for bounding over with room to spare. Precipitous peaks? Bag them by the daily dozen. And whereas the bighorn may not match the dazzling speed of the deer or pronghorn, it more than compensates by way of an uncanny access to the third dimension of material existence. With all its courage and physical brilliance in the vertiginous realm where mountains meet sky, the Sierra bighorn may as well have wings.

The Sierra bighorn, *Ovis canadensis sierrae*, dwells only in the Sierra Nevada. Considered a genetically distinct subspecies of the bighorn sheep known across the montane regions of the North American West, the Sierra bighorn's most conspicuous outward distinction is found in horns of the ram, which corkscrew outward from the animal's head in a broad spiral, splaying more widely than those of its desert and Rocky Mountain relatives. The horns are composed of a spongy shock-absorbing core of bone sheathed in flexible, spring-like keratin, the same durable material found in the animals' superbly adapted hooves, and for that matter in the claws and talons (and fingernails) of its predators. Horns grow throughout the animal's life, and each year a new section forms at its base, adding length and girth. One can roughly estimate a ram's age by the number of deep grooves demarcating the horn's annual growth rings.

The horns of a mature ram might weigh thirty pounds—as much as the animal's entire skeleton. Rams deploy this formidable weaponry in fierce contests to establish dominance. During the late autumnal rut, hormones surge through the ram's blood, sharpening a need for clarity, of knowing just exactly where one stands among one's brethren. Rams challenge their rivals with aggressive kicks and neck wrestling contests, even taunting them with flicks of their indigo tongues. If a score can't be settled quickly, the sheep will come to blows. Rearing up on their hind legs, they charge, falling into one another with heads clashing at speeds of more than twenty miles an hour. One such collision with a 250-pound ram would leave any one of us finished in an instant; yet the rams may go at it for the better part of a day, crashing into one another again and again, the sounds of each collision echoing like gunshots across the surround of lonely peaks.

Rams, remarkably, survive these impacts. In addition to having some shock absorption provided by their horns, the animals are able to squeeze blood into vessels that supply the brain, producing a kind of cranial bubble wrap that prevents the cerebrum from sloshing within the animal's double-layered skull. After each head-clanging collision, the rams face off and stare at one another, as if to say *have you had enough yet?* until one of them finally has. The stakes are high, for the victor of these contests will win access to a harem of receptive females. The defeated might still have a chance, but only if they can manage to employ more surreptitious means to arrange furtive couplings.

~ ~ ~

Mothers know in their bones that fate does not always smile upon the young. Bighorn sheep inhabit a landscape of fear, at least for any creature of ordinary sensibility. Death comes dressed in many cloaks—disease, starvation, snow avalanches, mountain lions, coyotes, golden eagles, or perhaps an unlucky ledge of rock that should have held. For millennia the Sierra bighorn thrived despite these difficulties, until the nineteenth century at least, when the introduction of domestic sheep, which brought new diseases and competition for forage, and increased hunting began to winnow the population of Sierra bighorn.

A few days before giving birth, an expectant ewe will leave her herd in search of refuge in some remote haunt of the range, perhaps the very site of her own emergence into the world. She seeks a place with proximity to steep escape routes and unbroken views of her surroundings so that with her sharp eyesight she might spy approaching predators long before they reach striking distance. For this sense of safety the ewe treads, metaphorically, on an edge, trading prospect for protection, forgoing access to the best quality forage (and the nutritious milk it would have supplied) to escape the depredations of coyotes and mountain lions. Still a newborn lamb might succumb to the attack of the golden eagle, who can readily carry it off on the wing. The young lamb's life is balanced on a pin. Only a few will survive past their second year.

Elders are vital to lambs' survival. Bighorn raised in herds with help from grandmotherly ewes, whose own lamb-bearing years have receded, ensure the next generation stands a better shot of making it to adulthood. No one knows exactly why. Call it matriarchal wisdom, practicality, and care. If a lamb, with crucial assistance at a vulnerable time in its young life, perseveres to adulthood—evading claws, talons, starvation, calamitous falls, bitter cold, bullets, assaults from microbes and parasites—it might live to fourteen years of age. And what a life in these short years, full of companionship and high adventure, full of rambling among mountaintop sky gardens, where from tender alpine grasses and flowers bloom dreams of a delicious survival.

~ ~ ~

Twenty years ago—near the time each of our daughters, Sophie and Gabriella, were born—the population of the Sierra bighorn had plummeted to a tenth of its historical abundance, spiraling perilously close to the edge of what ecologists call an extinction vortex. About a hundred individuals remained. Sierra bighorn had become so few in number that the accumulating effects of inbreeding, compounded by one or two bad years—be it in the form of increased predation, disease outbreak, a particularly brutal winter, or a drought resulting in low forage production—threatened to push the species past the edge of existence, to become forever gone. The bighorn's perilous situation catalyzed an aggressive recovery effort aimed at redistributing groups of Sierra bighorn from more established populations to smaller satellite herds disbursed over the range, with the hope of spreading out risk. Sheep were captured and relocated, with the aid of helicopters and netguns, by biologists with seriously epic mountaineering and sheep-wrangling skills. Part of the recovery effort also involved the highly controversial culling of mountain lions in areas of the range in which predation by lions had winnowed down numbers of reintroduced herds. The population of Sierra bighorn has responded to this ongoing endeavor, increasing as of this writing to about half of their historical abundance; though the future of the Sierra bighorn is nevertheless still precarious.

I cannot but hope there would be a way for both of our species, bighorn and human, to continue on our way, wandering and dreaming over high, lonely mountains of the Sierra Nevada. I can't help but feel some sense of deep kinship with this wild creature, this animal who edged back from extinction's cliff, with the concerted help of devoted individuals, during the very years our daughters learned to walk, then began to read and tell knock-knock jokes, then become close friends in high school. This Sierra bighorn must have high peaks and rugged rock and wide expanses of open sky if it is to thrive. I think I might need this too.

—RJN

We live in miracle when we witness a bighorn step along talus and navigate chasms, go blithely across rimrock or thread its way along a narrow peak, all with some uncanny combination of grace, balance, power, and derring-do. It is a showing of high spirits.

There is a certain jauntiness. The bighorn is a heavy animal. A long fall would likely be fatal. Yet they are able to face mortal danger with a potent animal faith that, whatever the terror of the risk, they will find solid ground. It is as if the bighorn has managed to unify itself with its habitat and transcend it at the same time.

From such rare attainment, what can we learn about the development of our minds? We see at once our similarity with the bighorn, for as the years pass we come to learn how our own lives are in danger every day. Many of us know how loss, at any moment, can sledgehammer a life. Yet, like the bighorn, we carry on despite our own confirmed fragility. We learn to cherish the uncertainties of the terrain. And somehow, we must make death an ally. Martin Luther King said, "If a man has not discovered something he will die for, he isn't fit to live." And this holds true not just in the struggle for justice but also in the minutiae of the decisions we make in ordinary life. We must risk ourselves, daily, personally, devotedly. And we can do so with grace, when we form a relation with death that is at once endlessly serious and uncontrollably playful.

> Death came by—
> A butterfly landed
> On his nose.
>
> Death came by—
> A murmuration of starlings
> Filled the house.
>
> Death came by—
> Decorously, since he
> Wanted a bourbon.
>
> Death came by—
> Put down his scythe,
> Had a hot tamale.
>
> Death came by—
> The cat melted him
> With nuzzling, purring.
>
> Death came by—
> The dog led him out
> To play fetch.
>
> Death came by—
> The children found out
> He was ticklish.

Death came by—
My daughter said she'd
Paint his toenails.

Death came by—
Said he'd give it up
To hear a cello.

Death came by—
Said no one had ever
Offered to kiss him.

Death came by—
Asked to look at all
The trail maps.

The bighorn offers another lustrous example of life by its ability to make solid ground, even out of a precipice. It makes of its own thoughtful forward motion an exercise of ebullient survival. How might we follow them in this way of thriving? We must always keep moving, even as we build our understanding of the world. The Sufis have invaluable proverbs on this theme: "A solved problem is as useful to us as a broken sword on a battlefield." We must never despair that our failures and misunderstandings, and the violence and fraud in the world, mean that we must be irrevocably deceived. As Rumi put it, "Counterfeiters exist because there is such a thing as real gold." We must carry on in the faith that our own rough and terrible limitations, in which we seal ourselves crudely away from beauty and our best labors and loving, can always be overcome. The Sufis again: "He who has made a door and a lock has also made a key."

And if we use that key, open ourselves to the world, keep moving and learning, then we can, like the bighorn, find ourselves on solid ground, wherever we may be.

Solid ground—
Everyone must make
Their own.

Solid ground—
One mountain plays with
All the others.

Solid ground—
Volcanoes and cool mountain springs
Make jokes together.

Solid ground—
Water reads aloud
  Books of the canyon.

Solid ground—
Music held in every stone,
  Every dust mote.

Solid ground—
Love is candor, phosphor,
  Stormfront of blessing.

Solid ground—
One leaf falls, the trajectory
  Of heaven.

Solid ground—
Words come together uncontrollably
  For a riff.

Solid ground—
Space and time meet
  To make love.

Solid ground—
Joy held inside all day:
  Soft tornado.

—SN

ASPEN

Populus Tremuloides

It's not that there's not enough beauty,
it's that there's so much of it, it can hardly be borne.

—Heather King

Look how the floor of heaven
Is thick inlaid with patines of bright gold:
There's not the smallest orb which thou behold'st
But in this motion like an angel sings

—Shakespeare

The memory of that momentary blaze, in fact, and the art that issued from
it, can become a kind of reproach to the fireless life in which you find your-
self most of the time.

—Christian Wiman

8/9/17, Day 7. Evening at Crabtree Meadow. Enchanted place. Confluence of Whitney and Crabtree Creeks, which loop and meander through the meadow. Spotted a few obsidian flakes on a walk around—debitage—people have been coming here forever. Dipped in cool water and sprawled out on a smooth erratic that looks like a stone frog idol. Watched the light play on the meadow and forest and mountains and clouds. Clouds tangerine then crimson then lavender then gray. Sophie and G frolic and laugh and dance like puppies in the evening light. Getting cold fast up here. A marmot family joined us for dinner.

Aspens grow in fur-thick groves along the stream banks of the Sierra's eastern escarpment. A hush of wind stirs the trees to a flickering of leaves as bright as coins. The light shatters against them, turns electric. The air holds the scent of cold, damp earth, stirs an unnamed longing. "There is another world," wrote the poet Paul Éluard, "and it is this one."

The form of the aspen's milieu is self-similar. It is a pattern of gathering: the thin mountain rills flow to an undulating creek; slender aspen branches converge to a single white trunk. And each leaf—each leaf for itself bears the tree's form in silhouette: from the leaf's serrated edge a filigree of veinlets coalesces to larger, tapering veins, and they to a single stem.

The leaf stem (or petiole) of most plants is round in cross section, rolling easily between the fingers, but the aspen's is as lean as a blade; it resists such absent-minded turning. For it is made for other purposes. The distinctive design of the aspen petiole—like an oar shaft flattened at right angles to the round paddle of its leaf—allows it to bend at the slightest provocation. It yields to each breath of wind, flexing and twisting as its perfect leaf pirouettes through the air. The petiole yields, then springs back. Back and forth, back and forth—each manifold petiole of the aspen, each myriad leaf quavering a thousand times over. The leaf shakes off nibbling caterpillars. It turns to avoid taking on too much light—so blazingly fierce in the rarified, high country sky. The aspen leaves turn, and shafts of light shiver through quick openings to leaves below. In this way, there is enough light for all.

When we wander through the green or gold of aspen light—or find the trees dressed in the spare silver of winter—we barely see the half of it. So much lies hidden from view. Below, in the earth's darkness, roots move in slow motion. An underground time lapse would reveal aspen roots writhing like snakes, wending their way through soil and around river stones, laying their claim to the streamside earth as months race past in seconds. If we could trace the roots' subterranean meandering, we could not distinguish where one tree's roots begin and those of another end. For the roots are of a single being, they are of a selfsame entity tangled in an inscrutable

Gordian knot. And the trees, which appear to be individuals above ground, are in fact shoots from the root mass below. Each individual tree might live for a century or so, until fire or disease or old age finally take its life to leave a sunny opening where shoots may spring from the mother root below. Each tree, by necessity, bears the briefest witness to the aspen's collective millennia of life. Each new shoot builds from what has preceded it, turns light to flesh, provides for what trees may come.

In the Eastern Sierra, copses of aspens thread their way up river canyons and avalanche chutes. In spring you can distinguish each aspen colony as it flowers and leafs out with its tiny, luminous leaves, all in unison. The trees grow verdant through summer and then in late September begin to acquire a nascent hint of lemony green. By October, hues of apple-gold and russet blaze in the mountainside groves.

As the trees sense the diminishing light of fall's shortening days, they begin a nearly month-long process of metamorphosis. It starts with a dismantling of the leaves' chloroplasts—the light-harvesting machinery in leaf cells—setting into motion a cascade of chemical and cellular transformations that prepares the leaf to give its nutrients to the body of the tree. When the leaf's work is finally done, a curtain of cork cells closes at the base of its petiole, sealing it off. The leaf withers, falls, draws its gold to the ground.

The turning of aspen leaves is an event of astronomical proportions. Consider that a mature aspen possesses leaves numbering in the tens of thousands, and that each aspen leaf consists of tens of millions of cells, and that each cell contains approximately forty emerald-hued chloroplasts. Such is the quantity of chloroplasts in a single aspen (when leafed out in all its voluptuous, green summer glory) that it exceeds the number of stars in our Milky Way one hundredfold.

That aspens give up their leaves each autumn, remake them anew in spring—a wonder in itself—is a transformation made even more wondrous by the fact that aspens are the only tree to elect such an energetically expensive life strategy in the Sierra high country—and still somehow thrive in its brief growing season. Consider the aspen's arboreal companions: the ubiquitous pines and firs of the Sierra, cloaked in their thick, corrugated bark, and their branches swathed in dark green needles clinging faithfully to their trees for several years—some for more than a decade. On a bluebird day after a snowstorm, a conifer's photosynthetic machinery can rev up for a few hours to take advantage of the brief, intense sunlight—and then when the spring sun returns in earnest, kick hard into action for the season. This begs the question of why the aspen should be the only deciduous tree to be found in the Sierra high country. The secret is in the aspen's skin: beneath the tree's thin, powdery-white layer of outer bark lies a pale green sheath of tissue that enables the tree to photosynthesize through the cold days of winter.

It is difficult to walk briskly through a grove of aspen, no matter what the season. The trees seem to want you to slow down and take notice. Even beneath the pewter of a winter sky, when the aspen forest is as bare as bones and the crooks of its branches are buttressed with snow, the trees sing life.

—RJN

All of us live at risk to a mortal danger: our minds, our souls, and our senses may die within us. Our bonds with life may cool and fray, so that our days pass without a kindling of ideas and thankfulness, but in withdrawal and isolation. We do not, in such failure, find any flourishing in sunlight, but merely bear witness to it, in a kind of deathwatch. There are many signs of such a state, but one of them would be a failure of readiness, of our ability to yield ourselves wholly to the strange, come-hither beauty of everyday events, in all their power, intricacy, and surprise.

Readiness is the centermost quality of the aspen leaves. The uncanny design of the petioles means that the least stirring of air will set the whole tree waving, searching, and turning, so that we can see the intricacies and travels of the wind. What is more, we are treated to a pattern of flashing as the leaves catch sunlight. The patterns ripple across one tree, then the whole grove of aspen, all along the hillside. In the autumn it is a resurgent golden offering. It is the cave of Ali Baba, brought suddenly into the light. It is teaching us: we must urgently learn to conduct ourselves in concord with the way of aspen. We need to make sure our minds open to the minute offerings and sweeping patterns in the hours and days. We need, to live, this consummate watchfulness and cherishing of our daily chances. If we cannot receive such gold, the loss is terrible, since then we will never be able to give it away.

That is not the only teaching: aspen show us as well the means of renewal. Sometimes we must recognize the need to transform our lives; that is, we need to die in one life so as to prepare for another. It happens through all our years. We have only to think how in parenting we are joyfully enveloped in years-long love and care, until our children leave to seek their own learning, in exuberant independence; how love may arrive and depart, and our lives change irrevocably and seismically; or how an initiative of work may rise within us, claim all our energies, and hold unprecedented joys. The aspen teaches us how to recognize when one life is over and another must come to birth. It is the moment we know we must give everything we have in hopes of an uncanny renewal of life.

> Then one day his life stopped. He
> Changed, as, say, plain rock you see

In space, changes into a ready planet
With oceans, numbers, cougars, wonders,
Jokes, ice cream, hope. He set

His life on a crooked course, that,
Though few understood, held within
A trust and blaze of light . . .

What else might the aspen teach? As we walk among the peaceable rampage of
the gold leaves, we see the trees one by one. But beneath our feet, the root system
weaves all the trunks together into one life. We walk among individual trees whose
unity is hidden, powerful, extraordinary, fateful. It is a unity directly related to a
central idea among the Sufis, the Unity of Revelation: the core of revealed religion
is an experience of knowledge and beauty that is always and everywhere the same.
And it is available to everyone. It is as if we are born to understand that learning,
love, earth, and revelation are all woven together.

If you would love, understand. If
You would live, stand forth to lift

Hands in thanksgiving. Here is earth.
We must undo darkness with a gift
Found in the canny sidereal church

Of every hour: go there, live there,
Because genesis is today: beginning
Within you. A wild point of care
Is revelation and revelation . . .

—SN

PAINTBRUSH

Castilleja

The good will of a flower
The Man who would possess
Must first present
Certificate
Of minted Holiness.

—Emily Dickinson

People from a planet without flowers would think we must be mad with joy
the whole time to have such things around us.

—Iris Murdoch

8/10/17, Day 8. Crabtree to Hitchcock Lakes Basin. Warm, lazy morning. Slow to leave this green meadow. Bath in the creek and a good cold soaking before heading out. 1,300-foot climb toward the base of Whitney, harder than it should be. Cheerful encouragement from chickadees. Skip past Guitar Lake and venture up a bit higher into Hitchcock Basin for the solitude. Barren here, the sky pure deep blue. We eat nestled among rocks. Famished. Early morning ascent to Whitney in a few hours. We prep all our gear, so we can wake up, dress and go.

What do we know of flowers? Of their wiliness and brilliance born of a ferocious will to live? Of their ability to extract what they need to survive over their fleeting lives, only so it can be given away? Consider the genus of flowering plants known as *Castilleja*, the paintbrushes. Species of *Castilleja* occur throughout the Sierra, from the oak savannas of the lowland foothills to the fragrant conifer forests of the mid-elevations to the sky gardens of the alpine fellfields—almost to the very crest of the range—blossoming in flames of vermillion and violet and cream and silvery mauve. Valley Tassels, Owl's-Clover, Wooly Indian Paintbrush, Great Red Indian Paintbrush, Hairy Indian Paintbrush, Subalpine Paintbrush, Alpine Paintbrush, to name just a few of more than a dozen species of *Castilleja* whose blossoms return each year to the mountains. The sheer variety of *Castilleja* species you might encounter in a single summer day of wandering the Sierra might be enough to make you weep with gratitude for all the world offers us. I, for one, know this to be true.

Yet there is so much that is strange, perhaps deceptive, about this gorgeous and varied genus of flowering plants. For instance, it's not the flowers' petals that give paintbrushes their colorful fireworks but rather their bracts—specialized leaves that grow underneath the petals. In most flowering plants they're various shades of green. In the *Castilleja* genus, the situation is reversed. It is the flowers who are green—inconspicuous, pale, almost diaphanous capsules tucked away within the sleeves of the showy bracts. There is something else, too, about the *Castilleja*, but it happens underground, hidden in darkness.

Should you let a paintbrush grow from seed and examine its unearthed roots, you would find them conspicuously short in comparison to those of other plants. For the job of a paintbrush's roots is not so much to independently mine the soil for what they need, but to find their way through subterranean blackness toward the roots of other plants. In this sense, the root of the paintbrush might be described more accurately as a haustorium, derived from the Latin *haustor*—one who drinks, one who takes in nourishment.

It is not entirely clear how the paintbrushes' haustoria find their way toward the roots of their hosts. Roots of most plants, perhaps following some sensory capacity akin to our animal sense of smell, purposefully eschew contact with roots of their neighbors in order to optimize access to nutrients and water. But the members of the *Castilleja* genus have reversed this strategy of avoidance and have learned, in an evolutionary sense, to seek communion. When the haustoria of the paintbrush reach the tender flesh of another plant's root, they enter. Two become one.

~ ~ ~

Once on a summer evening many years ago, Deborah and I were sitting in our backyard with our daughter, Sophie, still only an infant, the three of us rocking on a rickety wooden bench we'd picked up at a garage sale. Our baby nestled between us, all of us wrapped up in a big blanket in the cool California evening air. We'd just returned from our first trip as a family of three to the Sierra, watching ospreys pluck trout from lakes, napping beneath hushing pines and cloud-feathered skies—at night looking up at the Milky Way, our baby seeing it all for the first time. This was the beginning of a childhood that I'd dreamed of for our daughter since long before she'd been born—to have time among mountains and forests and birds and streams and stars and flowers. I wanted these things to somehow get down inside of her—to give her the kind of medicine and protection they'd given me, without my knowing I'd even needed it.

On this particular evening, the three of us were again looking up into the evening sky. Though we could only make out the brightest of the summer stars, we watched them flutter all the same. Then something slipped beneath Deb's shirt. And then a moment later, mine. Our little one, perhaps contemplating whatever dark sea she had traveled across to meet us, had, in quick succession, inserted her small fingers into each of our navels, anchoring home.

The interesting thing about children and the members of the *Castilleja* genus is that though they need nutrients from their hosts, they don't seek to harm them. This relationship is not a zero-sum game, every flower for itself. Rather, this relation is a collaboration: the paintbrush enables its host to lead a far more communal and big-hearted life than it ever could have alone.

The paintbrush takes, but it also gives back. Not just by way of offering food for pollinators and astonishing beauty for mountain wanderers. In the alpine flower gardens of the Sierra, the paintbrush's penchant for tapping into the roots of its neighbors is generative. If you take a step back for a moment, zooming out from just the relationship between the paintbrush and its host, and consider the alpine plant community in which they both live as a larger whole, the *Castilleja* engenders a richness of species more varied than would have been possible otherwise.

The paintbrushes, by drawing from host plants that might otherwise dominate the local floral neighborhood, diminish their hosts' tendency to overwhelm it and in so doing enable a more diverse variety of flowering species to flourish.

Moreover, the *Castilleja* is a native expert when it comes to concentrating nutrients—nutrients which are so notoriously in short supply in alpine eco-systems and would otherwise remain locked in soils or in the tissues of their host—and they give them back to their community. As the paintbrush senesces near summer's end, its withered leaves fall to the ground and decay, releasing an abundance of stored nourishment to the soil. In such a way the *Castilleja* regenerates its tiny universe, providing sustenance to myriad wriggling and green beings who must eke out such meager yet wondrous lives in the austere conditions of the Sierra's high elevations.

Wherever you chance upon a bloom of paintbrushes in a Sierra meadow, or along a mountain trail, or bursting out from some crack of rock, know they don't come into their dizzying arrays of color all alone. For we might understand the paintbrush and host as members of a family. And as with any family, there is always more going on beneath the surface. A giving and a taking. An ebb and a flow. An interdependence. A tender whole that is so much sweeter than the sum of its lonely parts.

—RJN

When we hiked through any portion of the Sierra rich in wildflowers—which was often—the surprise never lost its forcefulness. It was as if a door in the air had been thrown open to show us the first and best jewels of the world—the original and real jewels, of which the hard and hoarded kind are a mere imitation. And the treasury is that of the most abundant sensuality, combined with teaching both gentle and ebullient.

One of their teachings is central to all poetry everywhere, in any century. It is the deep spirit of the possible, of easy and infinite playfulness, that resides within language. This spirit, as with our conception of beauty, works through the prin-ciple of resemblance. When we examine the workings of our minds, we watch a current of distinctions, whereby the world is divided into different categories, clas-sifications, schemes, rankings, orders. This is true whether we are thinking of, say, rocks or flowers in the natural world, the nature and qualities of society and other people, styles and periods of art, or the various lines of inquiry and calculation in mathematics.

But there is another way of perception, native to poetry: to concentrate not on difference, but on affinity, so as to portray the hidden and evocative resemblance of things that are usually considered separate.

Let us look at the *Castilleja* flower: what do those ascendant sprays of flowers resemble? First, the color of the bracts mischievously colored like petals, in radiant scarlet: they look like a whirl of long late-evening clouds that have concentrated and softened the last of the light, so as to offer new texture and softness. They look like meteor showers, passing through space after being painted with incendiary care. They look like the bright turn and swirl of ideas all through our minds when, at our best moments as we work, ideas, memories, insights all flare together in a beautiful configuration, and we can see a fresh way forward in life. They look, in their lush red, like the passage of blood along new pathways in the brain, as we are changed, our minds are readied, and we begin to wonder whether we might dare to hope that we have gifts we might give away.

Patient attention to any element of the natural world—even a pebble—will set off, with time and affection, just such a wildfire of resemblances. It is the home-coming of the mind as it takes the world within, as we are unified with life; as we lose ourselves, and find ourselves, in the workings of the earth.

It leads one to certain questions:

When wildflowers come forth, do they cry out
In joy, beyond the range of our hearing?

Is each petal a new idea, new dream,
Proposition, overture, declaration?

Is that why they glisten uncontrollably
In the morning sunlight of midsummer?

Is that why they glisten even at night
During a new moon when there is no light?

And the petals, if we hold them,
Is it not all deliverance and offered cosmos?

Is that why we see daughters aglow, their ideas
All an exultation of petals?

Is that why we touch, smell, safeguard,
And treasure every petal, always, forever?

And when they disintegrate, is it because
of their living re-creation within us?

Is that why we have sudden resurgent brightness
In our reflections and musing and movement?

Isn't that just the resurgence of flowers who
Learn every summer of every original light?

Isn't that light what leads us as we walk
Along sky-high trails together?

Is that why all joy is a trustworthy,
Warm, radiant, savory envelopment?

Is that why we have a chance?

Our first, best, final, redemptive chance,
Here again, every summer, again?

Richard writes of another resemblance, between roots and the little hands of
his baby daughter. As we were led in our reflections, as we hiked toward a sense
of the unity of life, so did I often think of all we learn from the wild good luck of
being a parent. Watching our daughters as they went their lustrous way along the
trail, talking and musing and living in the homeland of their banter and laughter,
it was natural to remember my daughter as an infant. And with that memory came
the thought that if, now, I can learn at all, it is because of all that my daughter has
taught me, from her first days on earth.

Why does a baby seem to come here
Directly from another and better world?

Is it her little hands, ready to grasp
Your finger or to hold the planet?

Her infinitesimal toes, that cry out
To be kissed again and again?

The envelopment of her eyes, looking into you,
And through you to all time and space?

Her sleep, in which she returns immediately,
Wholeheartedly and deliciously to heaven?

Her smile, which makes us whole because,
It is joy, knowledge, and love all at once?

The way she is all soul, and only gradually
Comes to understand she has a body?

The way everything about her body
Makes her incredulous, even a sneeze?

And when she falls asleep in your arms,
Is she not offering you all heaven once again?

All of every heaven ever created, all of
Every heaven that will ever be created?

The hopefulness in her first steps, is she
Directed by her every dream?

Her first words, isn't it like the making
Of a galaxy in her mouth?

Her searching, endless, ebullient play,
Doesn't it mean all the earth is alive in her?

Are we not weightless with thankfulness,
To have a chance to hold her, to love her?

Is that weightlessness not the very presence
Of every wild good necessary promise of life?

Are they not our teachers, just the ones
We need for our own homecoming?

—SN

WHITEBARK AND NUTCRACKER
Pinus albicaulis and *Nucifraga columbiana*

Understand the whole through the assembly
Of minute earthly particulars.

—Shabistari

Sometimes in the summer I'd ride up into the high country and that black-and-white whatever bird up in the pines was always yakkety-yakkin', and flyin' in and outta the pines, and never stopped, and the thing was at *work*, Jesus, an' it always seemed like it knowed 'jes what it was doing, and I wish to hell I could be that sure about what I'm doin' anytime.

—A Nevada cowboy

8/11/17, Day 9. 2 AM. Can't sleep. Nerves, elevation, excitement, all of the above. Depart for the Whitney summit around 4:30 AM with G, Sophie, and Lucy, switch-backing up in the pre-dawn dark. Deb and Steve stay back in camp, both of Steve's legs going numb and Deb struggling with exposure and elevation. Exhilarating walk up the mountain—moon so bright I turned off my headlamp. After the turn at the trail junction, the girls bound ahead and make summit by sunrise. Sun comes up over hazy purple ridges of the Basin and Range—"Steve's country" Lucy called it—she is a torrent of energy, a dreamer, an adventuress. Freezing, gusty at the summit, we're laughing, giddy, shivering. Made tea and hot chocolate inside the summit hut and signed the register.

Venture through a forest archipelago at treeline. The air is sharp with the scent of whitebark pine, the only tree that grows in the highest elevations of the northern and central Sierra. In the sylvan islands, the whitebark's muscular trunks grow so close as to nearly entwine. The whitebark does not spread its limbs in the downswept, snowshedding convention of other pines. Its silver-white branches vault skyward and hold brushes of needles arranged in neat fascicles of five. The trees' dense stubs of cones, clustered among the bushy treetops, glisten with luminous beads of resin.

Study the ground about the whitebarks. What thin scrim of soil exists around their curving boles bears the litter of nut-brown needles and shattered, blunt cone bracts. Rarely will you find a whitebark cone even half intact. When, after having searched long enough, you finally find some fragmented, brittle relict, examine the parched, teardrop-shaped seeds it holds: they are trapped in a cone-cage that even the most vigorous shaking or hard-blown gust won't set free. And even if the seeds could escape, they lack the wings possessed by seeds of so many other pine species, wings that catch the wind and fly to soil favorable for setting down roots and flourishing. How does the whitebark, with its wingless seeds, establish life-nurturing stands at high elevation? Sit down beneath whitebark's boughs awhile, breathe in the Sierra's cool, clear air, and wait, with the patience of a seed, for its winged companion to arrive.

~ ~ ~

Should you fall asleep beneath the whitebark's branches, with the sky above bathed in moonlight and glittering with myriad stars of the Sierra night, you may be assured of a natural alarm clock. For once the pink light of the Sierra dawn glints the whitebarks' needles, the tree's companion, the Clark's Nutcracker—the raucous pine-crow of the high country—offers a wake-up call for free. At daybreak the nutcrackers rouse from their roosts, crying out in their harsh *kraaaks* and *craaaaws* from their perches. Aloft, they are ever garrulous, cawing to their mountain world. They are dark-eyed, handsome, formal birds, with robust bodies plumed in soft-gray down. They ride the air on pitch-black wings, white-fringed at their trailing edges.

The nutcracker's bill, long and slightly decurved, is as black as obsidian and as pointed and purposive as a sailor's fid. With this singular tool, the bird hammers the whitebark's pitch-bound cone until it shatters, revealing the nutritious, caloric seeds within. It is the nutcracker's beak that unlocks for us the whitebark's riddles: the upswept form of the tree's branches; its cone fortresses; the tree's wingless seeds; the pine's dispersal among groves of same-aged individuals, assembled in close company; and the very mystery of the whitebark's existence itself.

The nutcracker is the whitebark's wings, its ever faithful seed-bearer, its abiding orchardist. The tree thrives because a bird cares for it, and the bird thrives for the care of a tree. They are "made for each other," wrote the eminent biologist Ronald Lanner.

The nutcracker, after hammering loose the cone's tight-fisted grip on its store of pine nuts, pries them out and stashes them in a pouch beneath its tongue. It carries aloft up to one hundred whitebark pine nuts, a cargo amounting to more than a quarter of the bird's weight. It flies off and hides them among a constellation of caches scattered across miles of its high country territory. During the course of a single year, an adult nutcracker may harvest and cache some ninety thousand whitebark seeds. Months later, the bird returns to retrieve its hidden nut stashes, remembering their precise locations even when they've been covered by thick blankets of snow. Some seeds the bird leaves. Perhaps it forgets them. Or perhaps there is a larger imagination at work, just as with any good steward of the mountains. For who is to say what this wondrous bird is capable of?

The teardrop-shaped pine nuts that the nutcracker plants might flourish into a company of slender saplings. With long taproots, they reach deep down into rocky soil. Over patient centuries, they gain girth and stature, adding ring after thin ring in each brief High Sierra summer, reaching skyward with limber boughs until they too can hold high the tree's cones, sparkling with sap, where they might be easily spied by nutcrackers.

In their uncanny collaboration, the whitebark and nutcracker nurture more than just each other. Search the whitebarks' boles for woodpecker-hammered hollows. You may spy a pair of mountain bluebirds who've taken up residence, peeking out from the tree as they brood their pale, penny-sized eggs. Douglas squirrels chatter and leap among the branches, harvesting sticky cones. In a year of big storms, patches of corn snow abide in the crown's cool shadows into July, long after the Sierra has shed its winter coat. The snow melts in a trickle, threading damp webs among talus, making a midsummer offering to streams, bringing water and life to the bear and the frog; to the kingfisher and the thrush; to the dragonfly and to us.

—RJN

All of us stand in the sunlight and suffer storms. And like the whitebark pine, some of us find ourselves in rough countries and climates, in punishing conditions. Some of us must live through decades where each day can seem like a torrent of danger. It is beyond telling, what has been endured and what must be endured today, in a world that likes to claim, with such self-congratulation, that it has advanced splendidly by the clear lights of reason and technology. Yet we can witness every hour the way reason and technology are made to serve human depravity. Just to look around at random: the atrocity of the world's nuclear arsenals; the expertly designed celebrations of hatred in politics, in film, on television; the myriad forms of propaganda that besiege our lives; the centuries-long abominations of slavery and the turning of earth into a killing ground and trash bin; the venomous contempt of men for women throughout so much of our history; and, currently, the violent ruin of our privacy made possible by computers. To name these oppressions is a mere introduction to suffering.

To help confront this suffering—and our own suffering—we might call to mind a verse of Rumi, who teaches that, come what may, we are all ceaselessly attached to this life. And there is another useful Sufi proverb, "The candle burned the moth, but soon it will vanish in its own fat." In our work and life and love, we can rely upon intuition even in perilous times: Emily Dickinson, in her letters, wrote, "The sailor cannot see the North, but knows the needle can." And we need to refine our most subtle capacities for work—as Thoreau puts it in his journals, we must be able to extract nutrients out of a sand heap. We need our patience. We need, in dark historical moments, to see how time and nature might begin to heal the world. We must see that sometimes, to live means we must labor to salvage every chance, every day.

We think of the whitebark pine, standing in the light, strong through the storms, making cones that hold its seeds and its survival. A seed is a way to hold the history of the pine. It is a compact set of instructions sent to the future, meant to make life. To have a chance, it must be hidden and protected, and as the whitebark has its hard cones, we must invent our own ways to keep life safe. We make that safety by the work we do and the way we love. We make it by our homecoming to the uncanny, graceful workings of earth. And that safety, when earned over time with independence, in privacy, has a special quality: it is strengthened only when we share it, when we extend the circle of our lives to protect those we love, and the earth itself. Our project is to ready a life worth giving away, in hope to provoke a kindling and a flourishing of further life. It is as if we make seeds within the mind, in collaboration with nature.

> . . . As you give, so you must
> Be this composer of mind-stuff, alone
> And in company of the world. Use the dust
>
> You are. Wink and music, rain and light
> Everyone must compose day and night.

There comes a day when what we make needs the help of wings. We have to trust that, whatever happens, the world is on the side of life; that what we give will be accepted, be carried away. It will be safeguarded, according to a pattern of life that has developed over millennia, one so deep in the world that we can hardly see it. It is the hidden pattern of helpfulness, deep in the world, like the magnetic field, as Emily Dickinson knew. Like the whitebark with the nutcracker, we are visited when we wait, in faith, with what we have learned. When love and knowledge work in concert, we live in the certainty that we may entrust ourselves to a winged life. It is the way our own life can take root in the future. It shows us the paradox of all our years: everything will be taken from us, every single thing, except for what we have given.

> Nutcracker, where did you get those nacreous feathers?
> Do you fly off in dreams to eat pearls?
>
> So that they melt within you and make that soft luminosity?
>
> And those blue-black feathers, is that midnight mixing with lapis lazuli?
>
> Did you mine the sky?
>
> Whitebark, do you know about the twenty thousand seeds planted by your winged compatriot?
>
> Is that the reason for the grin deep within your bark?

Does it thrill you that you can serve her so many meals?

Whitebark and nutcracker, are you not the boon companions of the earth?

The winged and the rooted, in your blessing and bounty, showing how with mutual devotion life makes life, always and everywhere life—

—SN

PILEATED WOODPECKER

Dryocopus pileatus

It is generally agreeable to be in the company of individuals who are naturally animated and pleasant. For this reason, nothing can be more gratifying than the society of Woodpeckers in the forest.

—John James Audubon

Listen to that drumming! A woodpecker is the telegraph operator of the heavens, and when are we going to get the message?

—A Sierra hiker

8/11/17, Day 9. Back to Crabtree. Before breaking camp in the Hitchcock Basin, all of us nap after the early alpine ascent. I'm listless, only half dozing, mostly staring up at the unblinking blue eye of sky. We head back to Crabtree, taking a different route, end up walking through a boggy area with hungry mosquitoes. Deb doesn't even want to eat dinner. Finally I manage to convince her to eat and within half an hour she is herself again. We didn't pack enough salty stuff on this trip.

When the pileated woodpecker sets to its task, it sinks its curved, raptor-like claws into the bark of a tree, cocks back its body, and then, pivoting hard from the spring of its tail feathers, drives its bill home like a hammer. With the force of its entire body concentrated into the tapered point of its bill, the bird smacks into the bole with a resounding thud, sending displaced hunks of wood hurtling through the air. Imagine slamming your nose into a brick wall at sixteen miles an hour, because that's pretty much what this bird does for a living.

It is a wonder that the woodpecker, after one attempt at such heady work, does not fall unconscious from its perch, tumble backward to the ground, and then—should it survive—awake in a daze, renounce all expectations of its kind, and wander off to contemplate the mystery of being and write haikus. (Perhaps it is such arboreal encounters that explain much about the soul-nature of my dear friend Steve.) Yet the pileated woodpecker does not hesitate, it does not second-guess, it does not flinch from its commitment. The bird is all in.

Anatomy helps. Arching loops of muscle-sheathed bone, extending from the back of the woodpecker's tongue, wrap behind its skull and snap the brain case backward at the moment of collision to reduce the momentum of impact. Nictitating membranes flick over the eyes to shield them from splinters and prevent them from popping out of the bird's head. Meanwhile spongy tissue lining the front and back of its skull, along with a musculoskeletal architecture that routes shock waves beneath the cranium, dissipate the force of each collision and protect the bird's marvelously resilient brain.

Should you happen upon this gorgeous specimen of a bird—with its handsome black-and-white plumage and glorious red crest—while it is busy foraging, you will see it hammer again and again, dislodging masses of tree flesh until it finds its prize: a meal of carpenter ants or the squirming, gelatinous grub of a tree-boring beetle. Upon uncovering its quarry, the woodpecker whips out its pointed, barb-covered tongue, slicked with a sticky, glistening sheen of mucous, and licks in hot pursuit of its hapless prey. There is no escape.

The pileated woodpecker approaches the task of roost and nest excavation with the same vigor, chiseling out cavernous hollows into the trunks of dead or decaying trees until they can accommodate its crow-sized body along with several nestlings. The bird does not seem to mind the labor, for an individual pileated woodpecker will roost in numerous sites during the course of a few months, and monogamous pairs of pileated woodpeckers typically excavate a new nest cavity each year.

All of this industrious labor has profound effects on our forest. Numerous species of birds and mammals reside in the cavities abandoned by the woodpeckers—even pine martens and endangered fishers. The birds' prodigious foraging and excavation activities introduce fungal spores to dead or dying trees, facilitating their decay and the cycling of their nutrients into the forest soil. Woodpecker foraging exposes insects, making them both more accessible to other species of birds and more vulnerable to extremes of temperature, all of which help to regulate insect populations.

When you wander among the great, green, shady forests of the Sierra, watch for the hulking old snags of trees. They are the forests' dilapidated mansions, the venerable and charming historic manors in which woodpeckers—the brilliant, beautiful, industrious avian engineers of the woods—find sustenance and make their homes.

—RJN

All of us need protection, sustenance, and a place of refuge. To have them is our responsibility to ourselves, since otherwise we cannot survive. And it is our responsibility to others, since if we cannot survive we cannot serve our companions in life: our friends, lovers, mates, children; the neighbor across the street and a family of another culture and language at the antipode of the earth. We live here together, enveloped in the history and learning of humankind. That learning, as we live, shows us something more: our connection, every day, as we live, to all the life forms of earth—every one.

Watching the pileated woodpecker, we learn how to begin to exercise our responsibility. First: protect the mind. History is full of the vicious efforts of those who would oppress, attack, enslave, and kill for the sake of power and wealth. To do so, they must first damage the mind—the mind of each of us, slowly and methodically, one by one, until a culture of corrupt fantasy, fueled by deception and contempt, takes over a whole country. But this culture, whose method is propaganda and whose means is violence, must first infect the mind, if it is to make its infernal progress. What might be our protection?

We may not have exotically engineered muscles or specially composed spongy tissue around the brain. Yet we have a musculature of another order: respect for fact, a command of basic logic, insistence on clear language, a conscious development of the powers of perception, of insight, of intuition. We have our commitment to the rigors of learning and our responsibility to share what we know.

We have the knowledge that life without love and understanding is debased: a misery, a failure, a mayhem of damage. These are the muscles of the mind. They give us our advantage, when we confront, inevitably, men and women whose music is a clangor of hatred and whose bread is the chance to benefit from the suffering of others.

And we must do more than protect the mind: we must protect our eyes, as we work. In place of the woodpecker's handy nictitating membrane, we have another initiative. It is our daily labor to look straight ahead and do the hardest task of all: see what is right in front of us. If we can, then there is hope to protect with clarity and resolution the most compelling possibilities of life. We can try to work for deliverance, whether we are in a market in the middle of a rambunctious city or in a golden canyon in a wilderness full of strange beauty. We watch, we learn, in hopes of fortifying the defenses we have for our mind.

Finally, by such means, if we carry on with our labors, we might find sustenance and refuge. We might learn something of what we need to survive. We might begin to make ourselves a place to live—a place that, as time goes on, we can offer as a refuge to others.

It's a straightforward model we can be grateful for: protect the mind and eyes, do our work, and offer the yield of our lives to those we love and those who come after us. If we do our work, then we might open a way forward to a logic of life that is within nature and that offers us joy in proportion to our readiness.

And what could we do? To start,
Let a blue heron nest in our heart.

Let our sentences branch like canyons,
Our hands turn river currents, our walk
Have cougar and laughter as companions,

Our eyes shine with recovered dreams.
The world is more than what it seems.
The world is luminously what it means.
It means cinnamon, miracle, streams

Of starlight like a storyline at work,
Exultant within us. Love, we can talk
With granite and the tempest, can work

With ice shelf and molten rock, can
Walk among the stars, hand in hand.

—SN

BELDING'S GROUND SQUIRREL

Urocitellus beldingi

Fumigation using gas cartridges has shown to be 60% to 100% effective for Belding's ground squirrel management. Total costs, including labor for gas cartridges are ~$3.00/burrow opening vs. ~$1.00/burrow opening for aluminum phosphide. However, gas cartridges are not a restricted use material and can be used without a certified applicator's license (unlike aluminum phosphide).

The active ingredients of gas cartridges are sodium nitrate and charcoal; some also contain sulphur. This creates carbon monoxide (and sulphur dioxide if the cartridge contains sulphur) when ignited. This toxic gas displaces oxygen in the animals' bloodstream and results in death by asphyxiation. Gas cartridges can flare up and cause fire hazards in vegetation, so caution must be taken when using them, particularly in dry conditions to avoid wildfires and injuries to applicators.

—*Ground Squirrel Management in California: Best Management Practices*

8/12/17, Day 10. Crabtree Meadow to Rock Creek along the PCT [Pacific Crest Trail]. Plan is now to follow the PCT toward Soldier Lake and exit via the Golden Trout Wilderness. Simultaneously relieved and disappointed about our route change, disappointment mostly about not wanting this all to end. We linger again at Crabtree in the morning, soak up the sun. All of us in good spirits as we head out.

In summer the high-country meadow sings with finches' notes and sparrow tunes. Butterflies and bees weave among blooms of aster, lupine, and paintbrush. Everywhere the water rings round stones in trickling streams, and the scent of mud and earth infuse the air.

From beneath the meadow, a small creature—part fur ball, part lightning bolt—springs like a jack-in-the-box from its burrow, scurrying about to feast on seeds and flowers beneath the blue-bound mountain sky. Here and there it pauses to sniff the air, gazing out from its dark eyes to the meadow's greenness. In an instant, a seedy stalk of grass appears in the grip of its paws, then as quickly vanishes in a few deft snips of its incisors.

In August you might spy the just-weaned Belding's ground squirrel pups tussling and tumbling as their watchful mother looks on. If you hold very still, the boldest of the litter may inch over to inspect what strange and novel being has arrived in its home. Unable to resist, your eyes slide over to meet the young squirrel's curious gaze, but even the gentlest of movements sends it fleeing to its burrow.

There is good reason for such caution. Though life in a high country meadow might seem one of beatific idyll, nothing could be further from the truth. The Belding's calendar is marked by days of danger and seasons of deprivation, and the fleeting summer is no time to tarry. The squirrels must consume a year's worth of calories in the span of a few green months, gorging on vegetation as they watch the sky and meadow for movement. At dawn, their faces peek from their burrows. They wait, observant, twitching their noses, only emerging to forage once assured by the presence of kin that there will be enough of them to stand guard against the threats borne by talon and fang.

On sighting a raptor, a Belding's hurries for cover as it chirps out a high-pitched alarm call. Chaos erupts as the meadow explodes in a flurry of squirrels, each chirping and diving for protection into the nearest hole or stand of brush. On seeing a predator approach on foot, a female Belding's will sound an alarm to alert her kin nearby. Facing the invader, she posts on her hind paws and whistles her trill of staccato barks: *chee chee chee chee chee cheee.* As the guardian protects the lives of her relatives, she risks her own.

When in late summer the meadow turns to gold, the squirrels descend like tiny Persephones into their burrows, where they will spend months curled in silence beneath a blanket of snow. Cold and starvation kill many. Those that survive emerge from hibernation in late spring. Within weeks, each mature female comes into estrus for only a few hours on a single day. The squirrels make haste. Litters of five or so pups, often sired by several fathers, arrive about a month later. Each mother will nurse her young in a cozy, underground nest fashioned from soft roots and grass near the nesting burrows of female relatives. The mothers, between foraging and affirming their bonds of kinship with furry kisses, remain ever vigilant as they guard their young against predation, infanticide, and even cannibalism.

Despite all that claws away at any certainty of tomorrow, the Belding's ground squirrel prevails with a fierce, animal generosity. Such generosity outlasts the life of its giver. For the universe of a Sierra meadow only passes for a time beneath the squirrel's paws before it must be given over. Those who follow will each have their own years to live, to love, to hold close to this green, aching, flashing world. This world is ours, but only for a moment.

—RJN

None of us have control over the timing of our birth. And sometimes we are born into a place and a time that are incandescent with threats. Rather than the flashing of the falcon's wing that signals danger, it is the gloss of a political movement that might tempt us into peril; or bright, jeweled wealth that means to dazzle us with its malevolence; or a sparkling of finely constructed lies that hides a seething hatred. We might suffer the leaden weight of poverty or the violent imbecility of war.

When we suffer such threats, it means that we must adopt another way of life, one that has vigilance as its centermost responsibility. Just as the Belding's squirrel watches the woods for coyote and bobcat and the sky for raptors, if we live in a dark moment of danger then we must fine-tune our perceptions and understanding. If we do so, we can see how power may be malignant and wealth may not be a benefit to all of us but a weapon turned upon most of us. To have such perceptions, we can learn from the Belding's.

They are the maestros of survival. They know how to interpret shadows in the grass, a glint of light on the horizon, a brief tawny movement at the edge of the woods. They read the world, as they live, with an incendiary and continuous attention. They cannot be distracted. They cannot be deceived. They are grounded in fact, with a kind of ferocity of realism. They know where they are, what they must do, and how vigilance brings them to the blessed chance to care for those with whom they share their lives: their companions, offspring, community.

Learning from them, we can see what we must do in dark times. We can sound warnings, offer protection, make together a place of safety, and find the sustenance we need in our season of warm sunlight. To take on these responsibilities, in such times, is nothing more or less than to seek the special form, perhaps the unprecedented form, that love must take in these times if we are to survive. If any possibility of love is kept alive, then every possibility, as time goes on, stays alive.

If we can survive in this way, then at the moment when darkness and cold comes for us, we have the strength and knowledge to make a refuge where we together can be safe. And we need to offer so powerful a capacity to nurture our young that we can care for them, if need be, in absolute darkness. There, they will have softness, warmth and the yield of the foraging we have done for them, when we prepare for both darkness and the sunlight to come.

We remember the summer meadow. We keep alive the hope that we will have our chance to live in the grace-giving sunlight and the lush grass, the time of petals, birdsong, and the making of seeds.

We stay alive for one another. We stay alive because we know that, whatever the threats we face, we can trust that the day will come when we will have our chance to learn from the iridescent beauty present everywhere before us—to learn that beauty is homecoming. We must always be in readiness and in reverence before animal life, since animals can see what is missing from our minds. As they live, wherever they live, they sound the grace notes of reality.

Because they belong here, unlike us.
Because they adore both the dust

And myriad rainbows on the rapids
Of a wild river; both lapis tambourine
Of ocean along the shore, and catydids

Whose song colors the sky, whose wings
Like everyone's, live inside music. We
Know animals love, because even to see
Them, is our grace. Is blessing. Kings

And princes, generals, presidents, are
No match for a fateful operatic sheen
On dragonfly wings, for the soft star

Of warmth in a winter den. Do you accept us?
Heart's whole journey is to earn your trust.

—SN

MOUNTAIN CHICKADEE

Poecile gambeli

Every form on earth is a self-disclosure
of the Divine.

—Shabistari

I realized that If I had to choose, I would rather have birds than airplanes.

—Charles Lindbergh

8/12/17, Day 10. Walk to Rock Creek. We traversed through open, stubbly foxtail-lodgepole forest over rolling terrain. Soil is rocky, thin, barren, gravelly—barely formed, reflecting dry heat. Nosebleed day. Reach the pass on the shoulder of Mount Guyot at around 11,000 feet—we follow the switchbacks down the other side, Steve and I hang back, walk through tree shadows. We muse about natural history and favorite books and poets and the idea of writing some essays and poetry to celebrate these mountains.

Winter is quiet in the Sierra high country. The world is cold and hushed. Snow lays a white pelt across the land; it gathers in the pine and fir needles, bends branches to the brumal earth. Windswept spindrift glints like glass. The bank willows' branches, russet and ember-gold, blossom with frost flowers. Ice-sheathed streams, silent and slow, drift in an underworld of indigo. The birds, their music so sweet and raucous in summer, have gone. The air is thin with their absence.

But the mountain chickadee, winter's bandit-masked thief, remains. In the snowy, silent depths of Sierra winters, they hop and flit and glean, performing like playground show-offs among the conifer branches. They call out in their husky, harsh-sweet voices, scolding and singing *hey sweetie* and *fee bee* and *chicka dee dee dee*, as if it were some morning in July. With their bright banter and cheerful cascading notes, we can count on the chickadees to lift the heart of any snow-numbed traveler. Yet what do we know of what these winged mountain spirits sing for themselves?

Using sophisticated acoustic analyses, observant biologists have learned that the songs of mountain chickadees at higher elevations are different—in the timing and frequency of their notes—from the songs of their kin dwelling lower down. Such distinctions may signal to prospective mates their fitness for the rigors of high country living. In addition, the high elevation mountain chickadee's hippocampus—a region of the brain associated with spatial memory—is larger and more neuron-dense than that of its lowland relative, giving them a superior ability to find cached stores of seed—a life-saving skill at high elevations where conditions are harshest.

Walking through the forest on a calm, cold, bluebird morning following a snowstorm, you might spy a mountain chickadee warming itself on a sunny perch, then leap off and forage while its companions feed upside-down from snow-laden branches nearby. And on numbing and frigid days, you might find the tiny birds—weighing no more than a couple of grapes—puffing out their feathers as they move slowly and quietly about their work of gathering food. At night when the temperature plummets, they insulate themselves among conifer needles or bark, and tuck their heads into their feathers for warmth. The birds' body temperatures cool by several degrees, so that they might conserve energy through long hours of darkness.

Should you wander through the snow of a February forest at night, just to see bright winter constellations turn through bare branches of aspen, the cold would soon send you away, back to the waiting warmth of your sleeping bag. Crunching across hard crusted snow, the quiet world would shimmer with starlight. And tiny avian companions, tucked away in their cozy roosts, dreaming their chickadee dreams, would sing to you in morning.

—RJN

Everyone in the course of their lives will have to confront the facts of human depravity. The centuries hold finely planned mass exterminations and repugnant torture; they hold boiling contempt for others because of race, faith, or gender. There is nothing that one man—it is almost always a man—will not do to another. And beyond our personal violence, we carry on with our savage assault on the planet—as if, daily and inexplicably, we were a family working brutishly to rip down our own house.

We are killing each other. It is as if a flammable current of hatred inside history is about to ignite and engulf us all. These days, the current runs wide and deep and everywhere.

Each of us must decide what to do with this darkness, which is a darkness inside all of us. It can take so many forms: indifference, envy, ignorance; impatience, greed, anger; and in some people, a seething joy in seeing other people suffer and die.

As we work to undo the darkness in ourselves and learn what help we might give, we need solace and guidance. And there is no guidance like the lustrous working of the natural world.

The chickadee, with its rakish eye stripe and uncontrollably joyful song, is just like the improbable life that moves in us when things are at their worst. If we listen, we can attend to an interior world that holds and concentrates all the beauties of the natural world. It is what we were born with. It is what we can nourish and strengthen and redeem. If we have a place to stand on earth, we have a place to stand in life.

One way to find faith is to try to find the wildness in any place—even our own backyards—and to begin a devoted, thoughtful, patient engagement with that place. We see how trampled grass springs back to life. Or if we can find our way to a desert, we might see that a golden eagle aloft on the spiraling column of heat has an analog within us: we can learn how in the heat of events to open our wings and gain altitude and perspective. Or if we seek out a river canyon, we can see in the torrents of a spring river the way forward in our work, with just that cut-loose energy and beautiful momentum.

And we can learn how, in the season of darkness and cold, there is within us a movement of life. It is like the chickadee, small and playful, irrepressible and resourceful; the source of a fateful song full of whimsy and sweetness that beckons us to our better selves and to a better world.

This is, like every time, our time. We cannot wait to act in favor of life. We cannot wait even one further half-second.

> The stream of destiny
> Surges around you—
> Do it now.

> Every beautiful animal
> Is watching—
> Do it now.

> Light the fuse
> Of surprise—
> Do it now.

> Every clock stops
> To wait—
> Do it now.

> Door open today
> Never open again—
> Do it now.

> All weapons on earth
> Will melt—
> Do it now.

> In you a maternity ward
> Of newborn stars—
> Do it now.

> Life is a lens,
> Look for heaven—
> Do it now.

> Light the fire to burn
> Who you were—
> Do it now.

All your dreams
Need you—
    Do it now.

Sunlight never stopped
Searching for you—
    Do it now.

A whole orchestra
Awaits your music—
    Do it now.

Little birdsong,
Cosmic good luck—
    Do it now.

A handful of sand
Elixir of life—
    Do it now.

Stardust in you
Kindles—
    Do it now.

In you seasons, continents,
Justice, rapture—
    Do it now.

All your love, even if
For a single insect—
    Do it now.

—SN

MOUNTAIN YELLOW-LEGGED FROG

Rana sierrae and *Rana mucosa*

The wisdom spread through the sphere of the universe is no greater than the wisdom contained in the tiniest of animals.

—Milorad Pavic

To keep every cog and wheel is the first precaution of intelligent tinkering.

—Aldo Leopold

8/13/17, Day 11. Rock Creek to Soldier Lake. Last night we made a fire and sang songs and told stories. Deb's animate unforgettable voice. Our two families in the middle of nowhere, in this immense enveloping mountain range on a black summer night—one of the sweetest moments of the trip. Watched the embers of the fire burn down, then walked to the creek, looked up at summer constellations glittering in their sky. Our little fire its own brief burning star in the darkness.

The Sierra Nevada high country is a land for gathering water, where bowls of hollowed stone hold lakes the color of sky. Lakes open to the unfolding and varied movement of clouds, and on clear nights to the lonely turning of the stars. Silver-threads of streams slip from lakes' morained edges. Water pours between stones, tumbles, falls, funnels to plunges, whirls into pools, scatters in ripples. Water rings, gulps, galumphs, hums, hushes all at once. Water sings. The water is singing now.

At the edge of a Sierra stream, wind brushes a meadow along its bank. Pine branches whisper among themselves, hiding small flocks of chickadees *seet-seeting* tiny bell notes. Cloud shadows darken the bare mountain slopes in the distance. A smooth cobble rests in the shallows of the stream, warms itself in the afternoon sun. At the stone's submerged edge sits a frog, as small as a baby's hand, as still as a Buddha. Had you not looked carefully you might have mistaken this diminutive amphibious bodhisattva for a rock.

Study the form of this frog: her long hind legs fold beneath her, tapering to fans of slender toes draped over a twig. Delicate knobs texture her speckled back. Smooth, turmeric-hued skin rounds the beatific bowl of her belly. Her eyes peek just above the water, their irises glittered with flecks of green-gold and black. If you didn't know better, you might say that this frog is smiling. Sneak close enough and you might notice a faint scent redolent of garlic.

She is the mountain yellow-legged frog—a frog of two species found in the high, clear streams and lakes speckling the Range of Light. *Rana sierrae* dwells in the Sierra north of Mather Pass and the Monarch Divide; whereas her sister species, the longer legged *Rana mucosa*, inhabits the range to the south—and a few pocket-sized refuges in California's Transverse and Peninsular Ranges.

A century ago, wanderers of the High Sierra encountered mountain yellow-legged frogs in such plentitude that a certain care and gentleness was required to avoid stepping on them. Even then, the frogs—once the Sierra's most abundant vertebrate—demanded a kind of benevolent attention. By the hundreds the frogs gathered among the high lakes and streams, spending summer days basking in the sun, swimming in sunlit shallows, embracing in the mud, devouring banquets of caddisfly and mayfly larvae, all while they remained watchful for garter snakes slithering through the meadow grass.

Meeting frogs above ten thousand feet dwelling with such apparent equanimity raises certain existential questions. For how can this frog, who lives a life so inextricably bound to liquid water, survive the Sierra's long and frigid winters?

Picture a lake-fringing patch of marsh, where in summertime, you might come upon a placid Sierra mountain yellow-legged frog resting in the afternoon sun— or gliding just below the surface of the lake beyond. Consider, though, that by January, a thick quilt of snow will lay upon the frozen lake and the open country about it. Trudge the lake's snowy perimeter, cross its ice-bound length, and you will catch neither sight nor sign of a single Sierra Nevada mountain yellow-legged frog. Yet they are present, hidden in the water beneath the lake's frozen surface—or perhaps nestled into cracks of rock or among stones beneath slow-moving streams sheathed by glazes of translucent ice.

The frogs wait in a torpor, biding their time for long months in aqueous darkness. Each day glows behind a pale scrim of ice; each night falls as black and cold as space. First-year tadpoles drift in dreams, scarcely moving but for the insistent rhythmic fluttering of their gills. They might overwinter two, maybe three more years before metamorphosing into full-grown frogs. Come spring though, the lakes and streams thaw. Frogs rejoin the land, they bound across crusts of snow in search of lakes nearby, seeking their turquoise openings and companions who might gather with them there.

~ ~ ~

The ice-hollowed and moraine-dammed bowls that hold the Sierra's myriad lakes are, like its many precipitously walled valleys, part of the range's glacial legacy. Once glaciers retreated, unbound skeins of high-country watercourses began tilting over cusps of ice-honed staircases and precipices, falling tens, sometimes hundreds of feet, shattering into clouds of rainbowed mist. Intrepid amphibians could navigate around these vertiginous cascades, trundling or hopping up workaround routes to reach and eventually inhabit virgin tarns and wetlands, but this remote aquatic habitat remained inaccessible to fish—who have yet to acquire the ability to launch themselves up waterfalls.

Yet we took it upon ourselves, beginning in the late nineteenth century, to enable various species of trout to circumvent the redoubtable topographic barriers honed by glaciers, undoing the patient work of millennia in a matter of decades. Whether ferried by bucket or coffeepot, or later dropped by the thousands from the holds of low-flying aircraft, fish entered the once inaccessible lakes of the Sierra Nevada high country. Upon their arrival, trout—as predators with a penchant for eating anything they can wrap their lips around—began unraveling the lakes' delicate aquatic ecology. Whole populations of yellow-legged frogs began to disappear as trout devoured aquatic invertebrates, the yellow-legged's primary food source, and preyed voraciously upon tadpoles. Knock-on effects rippled across the aquatic food web: plankton populations shifted, which altered the cycling of nutrients, which enabled algae production to increase, which hazed the lakes' famously crystal-clear waters. On land, garter snakes, who rely on the frogs as a choice dietary staple, began to decline. And the gray-crowned rosy-finch—a handsome mountaineer of a bird who haunts the Sierra's highest peaks—suffered as trout emptied lakes' larders. Like their amphibious neighbors, the finches depend on aquatic invertebrates for food and were relegated to scant pickings of benumbed insects from ice-fields and crusts of snow.

It seems innocent enough, plopping a fish in a lake. But was it? Too often, it seems, we manage to deploy our observational intelligence after the fact, as an exercise in forensics rather than in precautionary prudence. And I can't help but wonder if the practice of stocking the Sierra's lakes might have contributed to another, even more insidious threat to our beloved yellow-legged frogs.

In the 1970s biologists began finding scores of emaciated, dying, and dead frogs, their skin sloughing off their bodies, in streams and lakes of the Sierra Nevada. The cause, which wouldn't be discovered for at least two more decades, was the disease known as chytridiomycosis, or chytrid, a fungal infection that invades frogs' skin and kills by disrupting their ability to absorb nutrients, release toxins, and breathe, eventually leading to catastrophic organ failure and cardiac arrest. Chytrid is a global pandemic that has reduced populations of more than five hundred individual amphibian species, with ninety of those species likely extinct. As a result of chytrid, which piggybacked on the devastations caused by introduced trout, Sierra mountain yellow-legged frogs have disappeared from more than 90 percent of their historical range. Yet the mystery remains regarding how the deadly fungal pathogen that causes chytrid—which doesn't appear to be able survive for long outside of water and sure as heck can't swim up a waterfall—could have reached so many remote alpine lakes in the Sierra Nevada. Could the pathogen have found its way into trout hatcheries—and from there into the holds of aircraft used to bomb the Sierra's lakes with fry?

~ ~ ~

As with that of any disappearing species, the fate of the mountain yellow-legged frog raises a briar-patch of ethical questions—regarding our responsibility to prevent its total annihilation from the face of the planet and the cost of measures needed to do so relative to other achingly urgent environmental and humanitarian disasters. Yet the mountain yellow-legged frog's survival could not be more salient as we witness the catastrophic decline of populations of wild beings and the wholesale disappearance of species across the globe, with the loss being particularly acute in freshwater aquatic habitats.

The Range of Light offers us a chance to preserve some patch of wild for the world. And fortunately, it has been relatively easy to reverse some of the harm caused by trout introduction through efforts to remove fish from suites of lakes that they cannot readily repopulate. The mountain yellow-legged frogs respond quickly to such gestures, reoccupying the emancipated lakes, sometimes in droves. In one study conducted in several lakes in Kings Canyon National Park and the adjacent John Muir Wilderness, the density of frog populations increased twelve- to forty-fold within a few years of fish removal, and from these recovering populations, frogs began dispersing to surrounding lakes.

But the battle with chytrid continues. Some mountain yellow-legged frog populations have shown signs of evolving a kind of fragile resistance. Meanwhile a few devoted groups of researchers endeavor to understand how to help frogs combat chytrid and tune strategies for conserving amphibian habitat, reintroducing healthy, lab-incubated, chytrid-resistant mountain yellow-legged frogs to areas of their ancestral range where they might thrive once again. It seems to me, at least, that such efforts of repairing the world, as they are done with great care, are as practical as they are sacred.

~ ~ ~

In spring, the high country meadows of the Sierra are glazed with clear, crystalline, corn-snow crusts. The previous summer's grass and sedges are brown and matted, pressed to earth like coils of old hemp. The world smells of mud and rain. Rivulets of meltwater trickle and braid over the meadows, transformed for a time to sopping wetlands. Water gathers to streams rippling cold over amber-eyed cobbles. Search with care among the stones and you might find a cluster of a hundred or so small, clear eggs shivering in the current. In the center of each jellied egg is a tiny sphere, as black as a pupil, as black as night.

—RJN

There is in the Buddhist tradition an established form of meditation, in which we sit quietly and, while the mind runs on, concentrate on our breath: its pattern, depth, pacing, nature. And we begin to watch the mind as it visits us with its thousands of impulses, connections, flights of imagination, memories, sorrows, needs, associations, pains, and longing . . . all the slow burn of our lives. The key is not to be distracted by this unruly flow but to let it run, to refuse to dwell on any one element, and to bring the attention always back to the breath. The idea is to develop the capacity for detachment, for inner awareness, and for a movement of life to the other side of suffering. The hope is to connect with a power resident in the mind for peace, lovingkindness, acceptance, and compassion.

There has been so much beautiful verse written in the Buddhist tradition, and preeminent among the forms used is haiku, the legendary Japanese form. Much of this poetry can be understood in relation to the practice of meditation, since it allows the mind to move past suffering to the plain, redemptive intensity of the present world, with its offered beauties and simple infinities.

Among the haiku masters is my favorite, Kobayashi Issa, who lived a life of inconceivable tragedy: he suffered horrific child abuse and lifelong poverty, three of his children died as infants, and one beloved wife died in childbirth. Late in life his house was destroyed by fire. After taking refuge in a ramshackle hut, he was struck by illness that left him paralyzed, helpless, and in pain.

His response to the tragedies of this life was to write thousands of the most transcendently beautiful—and some of the funniest—haiku in all history. He wrote them, at times, about insects, butterflies, sparrows, fleas. And he had, for all his solemn Buddhism, the most refreshing irreverence:

> From the Great Buddha's
> great nose, a swallow
> comes gliding out.

> Smiling serenely,
> The Buddha gently points to
> A little stinkworm.

What on earth, you may ask, does all of this have to do with the mountain yellow-legged frog? Everything, it turns out. Part of the method followed in the mountains by Richard and me is in effect a practice of meditation. But instead of concentrating on the breath, we have chosen the elements and life forms of the Sierra.

If we give all of our attention to the frog, what do we see, what might we learn, how might we understand anew the world? What if we gaze upon her, notice every detail of her beauty, see how she glistens in the sun; what if we exclaim at her capacity to wait in patience, semi-frozen, all through the months of crushing snow, only to gather with her compatriots in their homeland, all of them gleaming in the spring light? What if we make this little frog the centermost of our attention and devotion? Might we be granted the fortunate chance to come into playful unity with her life?

In such meditations, we find that the frog delivers us directly to playfulness, and to explore the world that she is we must segue from haiku into another form: poetry in the form of questions:

> Who is it that hammered those thin,
> Incandescent gold plates for your breast?
>
> And who painted the lovely
> Chocolate dots on your back?
>
> And those muscular legs! Do you
> Jump through the arc of the crescent moon?
>
> You're looking rather smug—is it
> The fancy black tattoos on your forearms?
>
> And all around the deep-space darkness
> Of your pupils, golden irises, really?
>
> Don't you think that's going too far?
>
> Those really rather svelte and supple toes—
> Have you thought of being a monkey?
>
> Do you love to hunt in early light, and
> Late light, so that even the flies are golden?
>
> And were you born knowing how to thrive
> Always in your own empire of stillness?
>
> When, on a lake under the full moon, will
> All the water glow with your gathered flashing?

We live in the faith that we can with our cherishing come into unity with any form of life. The more humble the form, the more magnificent the reality it reveals.
Issa knew this:

> My little sparrow,
> You too now are motherless—
> Come play with me!

The distant mountains
Are reflected in the eyes
Of the dragonfly.

Beginning to rain—
The old toad wipes his brow
With the back of his hand.

—SN

WESTERN TANAGER

Piranga ludoviciana

It soars—and shifts—and whirls—
And measures with the clouds . . .

—Emily Dickinson

Every living thing has the same wish to flourish again and again. Beyond
that, our differences are quibbles.

—Craig Childs

8/14/17, Day 12. Soldier Lake Layover Day, lazy afternoon. Spent the day observing the russets and ruby reds of the foxtails and exposed gold heartwood of lodgepoles. Twice I've seen a golden eagle catching thermals, gliding over the rim of rocks to the north of the lake on the skirt of Mount Langley. Rippling water. Bats skim the lake. At night the girls riff and giggle inside their tent for hours. A good way to live. Watched the stars and the Milky Way, the whole array turning behind the black silhouettes of branches and needle tufts.

There is a German word, *zugunruhe*, which means a migratory restlessness, an anxious need to get up and move—and if you're a bird, to beat your wings and fly. *Zugunruhe* is a desire and a longing, a need, a biological imperative, a pull on the body by an invisible force. Consider the effect of this force on a small flame of a songbird—the western tanager. The bird is a seasonal migrant to the Sierra, who when compelled, perhaps by some reason of lengthening day or changing angle of sun, lofts its small, feathered body up into the sky from its wintering home among the altitudinous pine-oak woodlands of Mexico and Central America and heads northward. The bird travels by night, variably alone or in pairs or small flocks, navigating by starlight through high, rarefied air, journeying north through dark skies in an annual pilgrimage of more than a thousand miles to the forested heart of the Sierra Nevada.

Upon arrival, the birds claim their territory, announcing their presence with burry, robin-like songs called out from branches in the Sierra's conifer forests. They sing with questioning phrases—*cher'-we?, chee'-we?, chir'-ru?, zee'-wer?*—from shady perches, hidden among the needles of tall conifers. The tanagers are surreptitious birds, more easily heard than seen, moving gently and deliberately, almost shyly among the limbs of trees. Many have described the tanager's behavior as subdued, even sluggish. Yet one cannot help but wonder if this just might be a learned wariness of being too beautiful.

When tanagers are spotted among the dun umbers and greens of the Sierra's conifer forest, it as though Christmastime suddenly and miraculously arrived in the midst of summer, decorating the pines and firs with feathered ornaments. The male tanagers' bright coloring, especially that of their summer breeding plumage, is quite the opposite of camouflage. Their bodies and wings are boldly patterned with black, white, and a luminous canary yellow. Their faces are dipped in an incandescent blush of red-orange, which the birds acquire from rhodoxanthin—a pigment possibly obtained from their meals of insects, who themselves extract the compound from meals of conifer needles. The male tanagers may be advertising brilliance in their prowess of the hunt—and their ability to provide for nestlings to come. Or perhaps they have evolved such vivid patterns of color simply because female western tanagers find it irresistibly sexy. Though we might swoon on seeing such a concentration of beauty distilled in this bright, feathered package of a bird, such vibrancy might too easily garner unwanted attention from sharp-eyed raptors of the forest—Cooper's or sharp-shinned hawks—who would just as soon devour the birds for a late lunch.

~ ~ ~

The tangers come to the Sierra to take sustenance from the bursts of abundant insect life and berries that arrive in late summer—and from this sustenance nurture their young. The female western tanager makes her nest—a small, loose cup of twigs woven with soft roots and grass and hair—high up in the branches of a conifer. She lays perhaps four eggs, each about the size of a small grape, each a pale hue of turquoise and decorated with a ring of umber splotches at the egg's blunt end. The parents feed their young with insects gleaned from bark or branches or snatched adroitly from the air while on the wing—even dragonflies, which they will soften up in their capable beaks before feeding them, head first, to their gaping-mouthed babies.

Yet danger lurks everywhere for the nestlings—from the predations of Steller's jays and nutcrackers; from owls and snakes and even bears; and too from female cowbirds. While tangers are out foraging, this so-called nest parasite will seize upon the parents' momentary absence and in secret she will lay a speckled egg among the unhatched brood. Some days later, a cowbird nestling will take eagerly from the tangers' offerings, freeloading on their provisions of food and child rearing services intended for their own.

~ ~ ~

Come late summer, the green of Sierra meadows fades to dun, and nights again turn chill. The mountains exhale. Life gradually and gently subsides to the foothills, to the Great Basin, to the burrow underground, to the shelter of a tree-bark crevice, to the tropical woodland half a world away. With shortening days the western tanager's compass turns south. The male's facial flush fades to just an ember of scarlet flame, and his canary-colored feathers dull to an almost oliveish yellow. Male and female of the species merge closer in appearance. Parents depart on the wing. The summer-fledged young will follow a few weeks later, pulled by the mysterious force of *zugunruhe* for the first time. The tangers take refuge in the deserts of the southwest, where they refuel, molt, and refresh their plumage before continuing on to wintering grounds of the high tropical woodlands of oak and pine, still a thousand miles farther south. Each western tanager may make the annual journey to the Sierra Nevada and back again to its wintering grounds perhaps eight times during the course of its fleeting life. What passes beneath the tanager as it migrates across starlit skies? Iron palisades that will never impede it, steel cages that will never imprison its young, barbed-wire stockades that will never fence it in.

Might we dare to imagine such migration, such freedom of movement for ourselves, for all our wild and human family? Do we not all need to find a safe home where we can thrive? Are we not, each in our own time, possessed by an aching *zugunruhe*? Does the universe not pull on each of us with a tug as familiar as thirst, as common as blood, as old as stars and stone and endless breath of Sierra sky?

—RJN

How do we name the joy that rises within us when we see a western tanager? It makes the mind sparkle, as if fireworks were about to be kindled there. The crimson head, the gilt oracular breast, the dark wings flecked with gold, their beautiful morning song, both peaceable and urgent: we see them and wonder how we might have such luck, as to be just there, just then, with her.

Richard writes of *zugunruhe*, the restless longing to move, to explore, to follow the stars to new ground. And the natural question arises: what migration might we undertake that would answer to our innermost need, our most clear calling, our shy and secret hopefulness? What is it that any of us hope for if not to make of our time on earth a source of life for those we love and for others—friends, strangers, and those we will never meet, even though our fates are woven together.

Part of the answer is a longing for place—for the Sierra, for a certain cabin in a river canyon, for a hardscrabble desert where we may see a cougar walking with effortless magnificence; for a mountain meadow where we might hear a tanager finish with a song its journey of a thousand miles. What can this one bird teach us? She breeds in the Sierra Nevada, and north to western Canada; and even as far south as the Four Corners in the American southwest. And then in winter, flies down to Mexico, and to Costa Rica, Honduras, El Salvador, all in tropical Central America.

We share with her this world. We have, like her, the chance to know both the temperate and the tropical forest. We have our own way of singing, of nesting, of caring for our young. Learning about her, we see the resemblance between us, the resonant affinity, the way we both need to make summer in the Sierra into a heartfelt homeland. And suddenly we know the migration, the interior movement, the longing that counts for us: it is the longing to yield ourselves, to lose ourselves in communion. It is our soul-deep, light-led need to see that we are not superior, not rulers, nor are we special, neither as a species nor as our separate selves. Instead we need the communion that is a beautiful undoing of our separate lives in favor of a blessed, wider, destined unity with the earth. Each of us must take on the work

recommended to us by the twelfth-century poet Hakim Sanai: "unself yourself."
The Sufis talk of *fana*: annihilation in the light of God. In the re-composition of
ourselves after so ardent and necessary a vanishing, we have a chance to fly with
the tanager, a chance for reverential adventure with life everywhere, whatever its
form.

> O falcon!
> My fingertips
>> On your wings—
>
> Cougar, at last
> In the afternoon,
>> We nap together.
>
> Hornets, may I
> Wear your nest
>> As a turban?
>
> Coyotes, count
> Me in. We'll caper
>> Through debutante balls.
>
> Bobcat, trust me
> I pray, to babysit
>> The kittens.
>
> Bat, take me
> With you for
>> Psychedelic acrobatics.
>
> Dragonfly, those
> Colors—are you
>> Professor of opals?
>
> Moth, your wings
> Unlock every one of
>> The doors of midnight.
>
> Water ouzel: gray,
> Small, plain, shy,
>> Packed with gods.

Owl: fierce,
Vigilant, predatory—
It's about joy.

Meadowlark: without
Your song, spring would
Stay home and sulk.

Hummingbird:
Sewing together the mind
We need.

—SN

SIERRA NEVADA PARNASSIAN

Parnassius behrii

When I stand among rare butterflies and their food plants . . . this is ecstasy . . . a momentary vacuum into which rushes all that I love, a sense of oneness with sun and stone, a thrill of gratitude to whom it may concern, perhaps to the contrapuntal genius of human fate or to the tender ghosts humoring a lucky mortal.

—Vladimir Nabokov

8/15/17, Day 13. Big day, last leg of the trip. Soldier Lake to New Army Pass to the Golden Trout Wilderness. Woke up in the middle of the night, watched the stars, felt blue, I'll miss walking through these mountains. In the morning light Steve and I muse over coffee, our delighted custom, before the others rustle awake in their sleeping bags. Felt strong after our rest day, with a light pack the switchbacking climb to New Army Pass almost effortless, like flying up over the edge of the world. View from the pass is glorious, I want to stay here forever watching cloud shadows. Finally, we switchback down what seems an almost vertical face of rock, then walk for the rest of the afternoon over a long dream of stones and lakes and clouds and creeks and green pines until we reach the trail's dusty end.

Come spring and summer butterflies roam the flowering fields of the Sierra Nevada. The scintillant presence of these strange, antennaed beings—as much as any granite monolith—give to the great range its lone character, its singular Sierra-ness. Consider a Sierra meadow on some bright summer afternoon. You will spy whole gatherings of butterflies turning spirals and spinning loop-de-loops in the air, riding swaying flowers that buck like mares. Devotees of the Sierra's butterfly fauna have found that more than 150 species inhabit the range, a biotic richness matching the Sierra's diversity of plant communities, which rise from the low foothill oak savannas to grassy subalpine meadows to stony fellfields skirting the mountaintops.

Some butterfly species dwell nowhere else in the world but in our Range of Light. Among these is the Sierra Nevada parnassian. To meet it you must venture to the mountains' high, treeless reaches, where you might come upon a male perched next to a mud puddle, licking salt—which he may give as a love-offering to his mate, if he is lucky enough to find one. Or you might spy one floating up a steep talus slope to a rocky ridgetop, then fall like a leaf over a cliff on its other side. Wander among the gardens of pincushion flowers, huddled close to lichened rocks for wind protection and warmth, and you may even find the parnassian's eggs. Adhered to stems or leaves, they resemble tiny skeletons of sea urchins crocheted from gossamer lace.

The eggs, after waiting out the long Sierra winter beneath quilts of snow, hatch into ink-black, hairy caterpillars in summer's short burst. The hatchlings make for the leafy rosettes of the stonecrop, a genus of fleshy succulents that have mastered the art of survival in extreme conditions, such as in pockets of thin, gravelly soil nestled among the Sierra's alpine granite outcrops. As the parnassian caterpillars gorge on their leafy diets, they accumulate a bitter organic compound called sarmentosin, a chemical relative of cyanide—which is produced in the plant kingdom uniquely by the stonecrop genus, and perhaps too by the crafty parnassian larvae themselves. As the caterpillars develop, rows of bright yellow bumps appear on their backs, informing would-be predators of their unsavory taste—or worse, of the poisonous, almond-scented hydrogen cyanide that sarmentosin produces should the caterpillars be munched. As if poison were not enough, the young parnassian possesses a defense organ known as an osmeterium, which looks something like a fleshy snake's tongue. When threatened, our wee hero will extend its osmeterium, simultaneously releasing a foul odor, the combination of which might be enough to scare the hell out of most would-be attackers. Yet the caterpillars feed in the full light of day, when their warning-light speckles alone might dissuade predation most effectively. When resting, they secret themselves under cover of leaf litter or stones.

The caterpillars eat until their bodies grow tumescent. Their skin can no longer contain them. So they slough it off, each caterpillar wriggling out of its too-tight wrapping, emerging with a more accommodating sheath of skin beneath. Soon the caterpillars outgrow these oversized coats too.

Despite their voracious appetites, the young parnassians cannot manage to consume quite enough calories during the short, high elevation summer to reach full maturation. So as autumn approaches they must descend into a second hibernation until Earth rounds to summer once again. They emerge ready to fashion a cocoon and complete their metamorphosis into adults.

Upon shedding its chrysalis, the adult Sierra Nevada parnassian bears a leonine ruff and a fuzzy coat of fur flocking the entirety of its black body, not unlike a polar bear, whose thick fur and black skin also help absorb and retain heat. Blood engorges the veins of the insect's wings, stiffening them for flight. The parnassian's wings are the color of buttercream, stamped with salmon-colored spots circled in black. Smoke- and charcoal-colored scallops pattern the wings' edges. Such striking designs, just as with the bright rows of yellow stipples of the Sierra Nevada parnassian's larvae, warn predators they had better think twice, lest they get a bitter mouthful of poison.

Though we pass through this world with the Sierra Nevada parnassian, the butterfly's experience of it—its *umvelt*—could hardly be more different from ours. They glide through their alpine gardens, navigating their mountain universe with compound eyes. They see beyond our vision into the ultraviolet range of the electromagnetic spectrum, sensing arrangements of petal coloration and geometric patterns imperceptible to our eyes. With their black-and-white striped antennae, they smell and taste and navigate as they roam from flower to flower and from flower to mate, bathed in an airy scent-sea rich with synesthetic information beyond the power of human imagining. With their long, black, tongue-like proboscises—which are a third of the creature's body length—they probe deeply into petal folds and imbibe aromatic floral nectars. Such an experience might leave us breathless, ready to shed our human skin, just so we might know again and again such intoxicating intimacy with flowers.

The Sierra Nevada parnassians might fly for the span of only a week, and in such time must find mates, lay eggs, all before their wings wear thin from the vagaries of wind and rain and from the sheer work of vigorous lives well lived in the harsh, high Sierra. The husks of their bodies fall to the earth, returning to the inchoate, alpine soil. They are buried with November's snow among roots and seeds and speck-sized butterfly eggs that lie in wait for summer's sun.

—RJN

There is a beautiful Spanish word: *querencia*. It means home, den, refuge, a place for life and loving, all in one melodious utterance. It is the one place we all search for. We recognize it when we find it: it's meant for us.

So it is with the parnassian, with its birth in the Sierra fellfields: it seeks and finds the stonecrop. There, it does two things we all must do: it finds the nutrition it needs in the place where it has been given life, and it finds a way to protect itself. The parnassian accumulates toxins that help keep it safe. We must find a form of conduct and a set of skills, physical and mental, that will keep ourselves safe; and these may take an unusual form, deep in our lives. We need to make those skills so much part of our constitution that they become attributes of soul.

It is most curious that such an effort is not straightforwardly taught. All of us will likely find ourselves vulnerable, and someone might well try to harm us; the variety of possible abuse scorches the imagination. In the poetry of Carolyn Forché there is the line, "There is nothing one man will not do to another." And beyond our physical risk, there is the violence called propaganda: the perversion of language in the service of power. Yet we are not taught to recognize propaganda, and so we are fatefully susceptible to it. And worst of all, there is the violence we do to ourselves, from our own laziness, heedlessness, self-hatred, and greed. Against all these risks, we need protection. And as we seek protection in our studies, in our work and love and search for spiritual clarity, we come to learn what at first is strange: the beauties of earth can make us dangerous to those who would harm us.

The earth teaches us to trust. We can trust that the power within beauty will give us the strength to change the way we are in the world; trust that we may undo our errors, our ignorance and detestable self-importance, and live anew. We can weave the years into a refuge with the energy of thankfulness, using as thread, say, the clear lines of light in the Sierra. And having a refuge means that we can use language with new vision, work with more uncanny energy, give ourselves until we are gone. In other words: we can ready ourselves for metamorphosis. Just as in the life of the parnassian, we may need to conceal ourselves, to retire within ourselves, to concentrate life within. If we can do so with trust, we may become trustworthy. And by such means we might return to one of the oldest dreams of philosophy and poetry: that within the transient world, there is a life-giving, grace-giving, permanent world we can understand. It is the movement, as in Plato, from the sensible to the intelligible world. It is, in the writings of Ibn Al-Arabi, the movement from the physical light of the sun to the celestial and formative light carried within that light, beckoning to us. It is a movement homeward to our *querencia*, at last.

We will know when we've learned: we'll have wings. And we'll know when we have them because we will be able to write and speak with clarity and surety and in concord with earth. The dream of language is the dream of life.

> . . . Nothing can destroy
> A good word given away forever to earth
>
> And to the one you love; because any phrase
> May be high jinx, offhand clearing of haze
> Around radiance of mind making a church
>
> Without enslavement and doctrine; because
> A book may call heaven close, a monsoon
> And animal music in her hands; because
>
> Language is made of wings. We will die
> Until the day, by this art, we learn to fly.

—SN

WOLF LICHEN
Letharia vulpina

A truly good book is something as wildly natural and primitive, mysterious and marvelous, ambrosial and fertile, as a fungus or lichen.

—Thoreau

8/16/17, Bishop, California, Looney Bean Café. Real coffee for the first time since we began our adventure on the other side of the range two weeks ago. God it tastes good and last night I slept so deeply like I haven't slept in months and months, maybe years actually—but I would put it all down right now to be back in the mountains, down inside the canyons, roaming ridgetops, listening to the creeks. I want to keep this place close, to hold within some scent or sound or birdsong, make it part of me, drink down mountain water, breathe in mountain air, feel the rough bark of old trees against my skin—Alive! I need to write this all down, to honor, to remember this place. Give me the words, please dear God give me the words. Steve is just now walking in through the door. We'll need to talk about this.

In the heart of the Sierra's red fir forest, wolf lichen clings to the old boles like thick fur, intensely chartreuse, almost incandescent. Used variably to kill, to heal, and to bestow beauty, wolf lichen lives for itself and brews poison for its protection. Though it cannot defend itself against toxins we emit into our air, it still sends a quiet warning.

Observe closely the delicate structure of wolf lichen: its small, twisting trunks ramify into tangled canopies of interlacing branchlets, as though each lichen body were a tiny, sprawling oak. Diminutive forests of luminescent wolf lichen clamber up rugged landscapes of bark, for the outer skin of a red fir is a miniature topography of corrugated, violet canyons winding among ruby ranges flecked with umber and rust. Though wolf lichen prefers the northern sides of trees, which tend to be cooler and moister, you can often find it thickly encasing branches in furry sleeves, or ringing boles with wreaths that mark healed-over sprouting sites of branches long since discarded.

Wolf lichen anchors firmly to the bark of mature firs. Yet for most everything else, the lichen relies on itself. Or, better said, the lichen relies on *themselves*. For lichens are a partnership of organisms—a fungus and a photosynthetic consort, a collaboration really—that fashions a communal being with a life more wondrous than either could achieve alone. The photosynthetic partner—either a cyanobacterium or an alga (as it is in wolf lichen)—produces food using sunlight. And for its part, the fungal partner builds the lichen's structure and harvests moisture and nutrients from rain and mist and air. A third co-conspirator in some lichen communes is yeast, a kind of microscopic fungi. In the wolf lichen partnership, yeast likely contributes by making vulpinic acid, the toxic, yellow-green compound that gives the lichen its ominous hue, provides a natural sunscreen, and shields it from herbivory by insects and mammals. Even hummingbirds, who fancy lichens as a decorative camouflage on their demitasse-sized nests, don't find wolf lichen to their liking.

People have nevertheless found numerous ingenious—if not always kind—uses for wolf lichen. In Scandinavia, the Sámi people used the lichen to poison wolves and foxes, hence its scientific name *Letharia vulpina*, relating to that which is lethal to foxes or makes them lethargic. Native peoples of western North America used preparations of wolf lichen for poisoning arrowheads, for treating various maladies of the skin and stomach, and for dyeing porcupine quills and yarns woven into vibrant basketry and textiles. The Tlingit of Alaska have used wolf-lichen to dye yarns a pale, anemone-green, which when interwoven with yarns colored in hues of turquoise, white, and umbrous brown, produce the striking zoomorphic and geometric designs of their ceremonial blankets.

Only recently have we begun to rediscover the healing potential of wolf lichen, in particular its superpowers in combatting cancer, metabolic diseases, and an antibiotic-resistant strain of bacteria, *Staphylococcus aureus*, one of the most common causes of hospital-acquired infections. The bacterium kills by sepsis, relentlessly spiraling through a loved one's body, shutting down one organ after the other.

Perhaps there is another kind of toxicity that the humble wolf lichen might help us resist—that of obliviousness to our own self-poisoning. Lichens are monitors and messengers. As they capture nutrients from the atmosphere, they do so indiscriminately, absorbing whatever airborne pollutants happen to fall upon them too. Sierra wolf lichens are bathed in a slew of wind-blown pesticides and pollutants produced by the incessant burning of fossil fuels. The lichens have tolerated these poisons so far. Their hardy persistence has enabled them to accumulate contaminants and thereby preserve records of pollutant deposition in Sierran forests, even as less pollution-tolerant relatives of the wolf lichen have likely declined in the range.

What is the forest? It is a web of relations—of light and trees and soil; of flying, crawling creatures; of fungal mycelia; and of clinging bodies of brilliantly hued lichen. The Sierra forest, every forest, is a kind of music, really, an improbable orchestral emergence, a song of life. When the strands in the web of forest relations stretch and break, the song diminishes. The world could fall silent. Might we at least attend to the warning that is whispered by wolf lichen, this bright companion with whom we cling to Earth?

—RJN

We all need somewhere to live on earth. We need a place where we can learn together.

Our support is the simple, necessary one: just as the wolf lichen relies on the bark of the fir for support, we rely on the physical world. Whether in the mountains, on the plains, or along a coast, we have as our holdfast the earth itself. We must answer the same question: how might we, in this very place, mindfully configure a life? How do we learn, what activity or contemplation would give us the best chance to live, to give, to understand?

What if, just now, rather than turn to volumes of philosophy, studies of psychology, or spiritual texts, we gave our attention to . . . the wolf lichen.

First, we can learn that we are not, as it were, ourselves. Just as the lichen is composed of cyanobacterial alga and a fungus, with the addition of a yeast, we ourselves are composed of a host of life forms. A considerable portion of our body weight—as much as 10 percent—is composed of bacteria. Our cell structure incorporates, richly and remarkably, the whole biological history of coordination and cooperation, of genetic change and community evolution, that has seen myriad forms of life through millennia. We have the most intimate and powerful bonds, always and everywhere, with all other life forms: we live in them, just as they live in us.

Wolf lichen offer this injunction: know how you are composed. Then take the next step and come to understand that none of us is alone. It is a physical fact that in the makeup of our bodies and at the root of the mind we are unified with all other life. Where might this fact lead us?

It leads us to consider the relation between beauty and unity. Across history, whatever the century or language or culture, we have seen how definitions of beauty include, as a central idea, unity. If we follow this idea into the domain of spirituality, to one of its most lustrous sources, we are led from the wolf lichen to one of the most potent ideas in the world. We are led, once again, to the idea of the eleventh-century Andalusian mystic Ibn Al-Arabi, who gave us the Unity of Revelation. It teaches us that the revelations of Abraham, of Muhammad, and of Jesus were the same revelation—a vision of divine order, of peace, of inclusion, of closeness to life. It is the revelation available to any of us, and it orients the mind as we learn to participate in the unity of life on earth. So does a physical fact lead to a spiritual initiative.

It is where we are led by the wolf lichen. It is where any real beauty leads, across centuries to a principle that may guide our reflections. It leads us to search for a life illuminated by understanding. It speaks to our hope to be transformed by a love that works on the side of life. Dante was right: beauty awakens the soul to action.

That is not the end of the wolf lichen's teaching. It works in the world in two other ways: making poison that protects it; and absorbing contaminants from the world around, to measure cumulatively the conditions of life. How might we trust the lessons offered? We have an obligation to protect one another and to protect ourselves. And we must take measured account of the dangers of the world: we call them out to one another and seek a remedy always and everywhere in favor of life.

Call it the practical and mystical expertise of the wolf lichen.

We hiked for days among the wolf lichen. Yet a gift is not less valuable because it is more abundant. And we were taught once again: every living thing, no matter how humble, can lead us to a beauty that is physical and soulful at once, sensual and spiritual at once. To be in unity within ourselves, we need to be in unity with the life outside ourselves. And beauty is:

Winsome lover in the bed of world, she
Is sweat and hope. With her pleasure, she

Bends rivers and paints wing feathers, she
Calls shooting stars across the sky, she
Passes her hand over the afternoon sea

And in the pattern of whitecaps touched
By sunlight, we find the treasure map
The mind needs, if we would see brushed
Into place, a future of grace. Any petty trap

In our daily life, she blows apart with
Her dynamite of mischief, first wild free
Uncanny play every day in the world, kiss

And sensual voltage of soul—we are sure:
We belong to beauty. Earth belongs to her.

—SN

EPILOGUE

We did nothing but take a walk in the mountains. We undertook our adventure because we needed to, because we could not and cannot live without the blessings offered there with such kaleidoscopic generosity.

How is it that any of us might understand such gifts? Richard and I, by the good graces of our friendship, wanted, simply enough, to honor the mountains where we were lucky enough to have a chance to ramble. It was on the long hike from Crabtree Meadow to Rock Creek that we began to muse together about making a book to share the life of the country we loved. And it was clear, as we talked, that we had a chance to bring together our different labors and outlooks. Richard is a formidable scientist and a celebrated teacher. I am a writer of poetry and fiction. As each of us had our own passionate and distinct cast of mind, the natural world came round to us with different form and meaning.

What might happen, we asked, if we brought the sciences together with poetry and spiritual texts, as if one could look through binoculars fitted with two completely different sets of lenses? Might it be possible to bring the qualities and elements of the Sierra into better focus, to see them in their grandeur and in their minutiae, to learn from them and their exquisite berth in the world?

Science is thought by some to be dry, technical, and quantitative. It is not. Study is exaltation. Fact is miracle. Number is portal. Understanding is joy.

Poetry and spirituality are thought by some to be abstract, ethereal, private. They are not. Nature is language. Mind is sensual. Soul is earth. Transcendence is practical.

Richard and I made two journeys: this long, thirteen-day hike along the High Sierra Trail, and the years-long interior journey to make this book for you.

Something of the savor of our journeywork is held in a dream I had two years after our hike, when I was camping overnight at Pyramid Lake, in the high desert of my home territory of northern Nevada. Pyramid is sacred to the Paiute, the Native people of the region. The lake is near the Sierra Nevada and every year is replenished by the Truckee River, which carries the overflow of Lake Tahoe, another sacred lake. So are the Sierra and the high desert linked, one jeweled refuge in communication with another.

That night, I had a dream. In that dream, we had undertaken another hike, this one in another century. Here is that story:

The water was as high as it might have been in 1800, and Richard and I were driving along a high ridge to the west of the lake, looking down upon its shimmering azure waters. It was a rough road; we were headed north, toward what is now the Smoke Creek Desert, but in the dream, as it would have been two hundred years ago, the whole desert awaiting us was a shallow, perfectly reflective lake.

It was slow going, but we finally made it over the north ridge and saw Smoke Creek and its mirror-like waters ahead of us. We stayed high; it was dangerous driving. At one point the road was covered in a foot of water, but we kept going, the water arcing off gracefully from our passage, and somehow made it through.

Soon the country got very green and wooded, and after a spell we came to a low lodge in the forest, all made of pine logs that had weathered to the color of brandy. It was very beautiful, and we stayed outside for a while just to look upon it.

When we went in, we saw a series of long tables, and upon each of them there were maps. At the end of one table sat a woman, reflective and composed, looking at us intently but with curiosity and a kind of mysterious friendship.

We told her that we were going to look at the maps and pick out some places to hike; and that we hoped she would tell us about those routes. She said, quietly, "Of course I will. It's what I am here for."

We looked over the maps and picked out three hikes, all of them in wooded and rocky canyons. Then we beckoned her over, and she looked at our choices and smiled. Then she looked at us a long time, and then said:

"The first is the Canyon with Shadows Who Teach."

"The second is the Canyon with Stones Who Know You."

Then she paused.

"And the third?" we asked.

She smiled and said: "The third is the Canyon Where Water Runs Uphill."

All we did is take a walk. But any walk can be a participation in the sacred. This is some of what we learned: miracle is common and daily.

We are, all of us, invited to earn a place on earth. And if we can do so, together, then love and knowledge will turn out to be words that mean the same thing.

—SN

ACKNOWLEDGMENTS

"Every book is a miracle," a friend reminded me as we sat talking on his porch, watching a beet-red sun sink behind the crest of the Sierra. As with so many miraculous things, it is only through the ongoing, sometimes invisible labor of many that a book might come into the world.

Nancy Louise Nevle, my mother, offered generous encouragement as she read early drafts of my essays. Her words kept me moving forward, and each conversation with her is a chance to learn from her wisdom, generosity, and grace. She and my father, Richard C. Nevle, now gone a decade, gave me two of the greatest gifts that parents might offer their child—time to roam among forests, beaches, rivers, mountains, bays, deserts, vacant lots, bayous, and starry skies; and a home, always, wherever we lived, with shelves full of books.

My family of writers at Stanford—Emily Polk, Rob Jackson, Lauren Oakes, Shannon Switzer Swanson, Tom Hayden, Russ Carpenter, and Liz Carlisle—have offered companionship and inspiration along the journey of writing this book, both through their own writing and their scores of insightful comments on early drafts of my essays, which helped give them their final form in this book. Among these writers, my soul sister, Emily Polk, has shown me—through the example of her own writing, teaching, parenting, and devotion to students—how I might strive to try to be a little better at what I do. Our friendship and ongoing collaboration is among the great joys of my life. In writing each of my essays, I felt that if I could somehow delight or move or surprise her with what I'd written, then I might be doing something right.

In the spring of 2019, I had the good fortune, thanks to a generous grant from Stanford University, to participate in a writing workshop in the Chiricahua Mountains sponsored by *Orion Magazine*. The workshop—as well as the time among the birds and trees and singing water of the singular sky island of the Chiricahuas—provided much needed space for reflection as well as inspiration, conversation, and writing. Craig Childs, a writer I have so long admired, was my teacher there. Craig's comments on an early draft of *Brokenness* persuaded me that I might be on to something with this piece, and by extension the book. I am indebted to Craig for the inspiration of his own gorgeous writing and for his generous and thoughtful comments on two drafts of our manuscript. I also wish to thank an anonymous reviewer whose insightful suggestions helped improve what is on offer here.

Since 2013, I've had the joy of getting to know a community of ranger naturalists based in Tuolumne Meadows of Yosemite National Park: Karen Amstutz, Margaret Eissler, Eric Smith, Brian Angelo Scavone, Kaleb Goff, Jack Mazza, Ryan Carlton, Yenyen Chan, Sally Lundgren, and Jean Redle. Their deep knowledge of the natural history of the Sierra Nevada and their abilities to draw on that knowledge to inform and inspire countless park visitors, including me, is a gift to the world. Observing their approach to natural history interpretation, in which deep observation, science, history, music, storytelling, and poetry are woven together, has both helped transform my teaching and informed the collaborative approach that Steven and I have taken in writing this book. Karen Amstutz has helped me cultivate an even more joyful and informed appreciation of our winged kin during the many times we've wandered together over high country trails near her summer roost in Tuolumne. Karen, as well as Brian Angelo Scavone, Kaleb Goff, and Jack Mazza, have each, at different times, reminded me how to get down on my hands and knees and look—really look—into the holy worlds contained within the petals of the Sierra's wildflowers. My essay on the western tanager was inspired by one of Kaleb's interpretive programs, as well as by a performance by a beloved former student of mine, Mayte Guerrero, in Tuolumne Meadows in the summer of 2019. The intrepid Ryan Carlton brought me to the scree-slope flower gardens in the Yosemite high country where the Sierra Nevada parnassians roam. It was with Ryan that I first saw this butterfly species, in one of the few places in the world in which it lives. Eric Smith's gorgeous songwriting, much of it inspired by the flora and fauna of the Sierra Nevada, showed me a way that I might, too, seek words to celebrate this place. Brian Angelo Scavone's poetic voice helped give me the words for something quiet inside myself—a way of being in and attending to the natural world that is essential to our spiritual—and ultimately our physical—survival. I am honored to call him a friend, a brother, and a teacher. Pete Devine, a naturalist with the Yosemite Conservancy, took me on an absolutely fabulous day of woodpecker stalking up in Yosemite and led me to my first pileated woodpecker sighting in the Sierra, an unforgettable moment that inspired the opening of my essay on this glorious bird.

I am grateful to Sarah Stock, who has so graciously allowed me to tag along on annual surveys of the park's high country butterfly populations, in which I have had opportunities to learn from several of the world's foremost experts on North American alpine butterfly ecology. Among them, Sean Schoville provided thoughtful suggestions on a draft of my essay on the Sierra Nevada parnassian, for which I am especially grateful. I also want to express my heartfelt gratitude to Andrea Adams, who provided insightful comments on an early draft of my essay on the Sierra Nevada mountain yellow-legged frog. I am also deeply grateful to the wildlife photographer Darren Cook not only for the way his gorgeous images celebrate the wonder of the natural world but also for bringing my attention to the audacious idea (his own) that we might choose to rename the Clark's nutcracker, a brilliant bird with ebony wings, in honor of York, an African American man who was both a vital member of the Lewis and Clark expedition and enslaved by Clark.

Among the many fortuitous miracles in the making of this book was an introduction made in 2019 by my friend Tom Fleischner to Kitty Liu, our editor at Cornell University Press. I liked Kitty immediately upon meeting her. Her enigmatic smile, offered in response to my attempt to describe the project that Steven and I had started working on, convinced me that an even richer collaboration might be possible. I was not wrong. Kitty encouraged us, early on in the writing, to include more of Steven's poetry and later to incorporate vignettes from journal entries I kept along our hike. These initiatives, among so many others of hers, breathed new energy into our book time and time again. I remain deeply indebted to Tom Fleischner not just for his introduction to Kitty but also for his own teaching, writing, and scholarship, which have inspired generations of students and contributed so much to revitalizing the practice of natural history. Tom's ideas and his powerful ways of expressing them have profoundly influenced my own thinking and writing about natural history. I also wish to thank Cindy Wilber and Rodolfo Dirzo, who first introduced me to the natural history and ecology of Stanford's Jasper Ridge Biological Preserve and invited me to participate in Jasper Ridge's teaching community. In so many ways, the writing of my essays in this book began as I learned from them how to begin to make sense of California's rich biodiversity in relation to geology and climate. My learning with them has helped me articulate a perception of life, land, air, water, and fire as facets of a larger whole.

Over many years, in addition to the companionship of trees and flowers and rivers and animals and mountains in the Sierra Nevada, I've had the blessed luck to enjoy the company of several beloved members of my own species. I've collaborated for many years in teaching a natural history field course based in the Sierra Nevada with Sara Cina, Ryan Petterson, Edward Rooks, and Mattias Lanas. I'm grateful to each of them for their companionship in the mountains and count myself lucky to have joined with them in sharing a place we love with scores of students over the years. I am particularly grateful to Mattias, who was willing to say yes when Steve and I asked him to illustrate this book. To watch Mattias draw is to see a man dance with line and form on the page, and the illustrations he created for this book conjure a sense of the joyfulness and mystery one finds in the Sierra itself. Ferdi Hingerl's infectious love of conifer trees and our conversations under brilliant stars and lightning bolts and rainy skies in the Sierra Nevada back-country have shaped what I have offered in writing about this place. Crossing the Sierra with Lucy Blake is to cross a range with a woman who holds a fire inside of her. Her indefatigable passion for conservation, can-do attitude, warmth, strategic brilliance, joyfulness, generosity, resilience, and thoughtful practicality are among only a few of the many qualities that I admire in her, but it is her friendship that I cherish most. Gabriella Nightingale, for whom the law of gravity is only a mere suggestion, is a second daughter. Her presence—in our family's kitchen, in our garden, in the mountains—always brings light.

Collaborating with Steven Nightingale, my backpacking companion and friend, has given me the chance to think with him about things that matter and to develop a deepening friendship as we traded ideas and words and dreams and jokes back and forth through our many conversations in the making of this book. Working with Steven is always more like play.

I'm profoundly indebted to the many students I have had the privilege to teach at Stanford, especially those of the Earth Systems Program, who've taught, challenged, and inspired me in countless ways. You know who you are. I have thought of you so many times as I have written the words on these pages. I thought of our conversations in my office, in classrooms, in the Y2E2 courtyard, at the COP21 in Paris, at divestment rallies on the Stanford quad, in a fairy ring of redwoods at Jasper Ridge, driving down Highway 395 beneath a big blue Eastern Sierra sky, hiking up Big Pine Creek, wandering through a grove of bristlecone pines on a cold spring day in the White Mountains, gazing up from the shore of a Sierra lake to a full moon, at tables where we have broken bread together, and yes, in the past year of the COVID-19 pandemic, on countless Zoom screens. As I have written these pages, I have thought of each one of you. I have prayed for the future we might work toward through our disparate endeavors in the world on behalf of social-environmental causes. May this book, somehow, fuse with your labor and move us closer toward a world in which we and our wild kin might have a greater chance to thrive.

I have camped and backpacked in the Sierra with my wife, Deborah Levoy, and our daughter, Sophie Nevle Levoy, every year since our Sophie was born. Being in this place together has made us the family we are—one that is more generous, more open to wonder and to beauty, more grateful, more joyful, more ready for what might come—than we would have been otherwise. Deborah's intelligence, creativity, artistry, passion, and compassion, and Sophie's brilliance, empathy, joy-fulness, and wicked sense of humor are like wildflowers that never stop bloom-ing. Your patience, acceptance, and support of me, despite all, is the greatest gift I could ever know. You are my greatest teachers. Somehow you have seen in me what I could not, and your love has given me the strength to reach toward the person I have longed to become. In addition to all of this, you are each insightful, discerning readers who have encouraged me to reach more deeply toward my intention as a writer. My heart overflows with gratitude to each of you. May each word I write be stamped with the love you have given. May each word be illuminated by your brilliance.

One last acknowledgement is in order. After so many years of wandering the mountains and forests and streams of the Sierra Nevada, I cannot help but be filled with a sense of presence of and deep gratitude to the Native peoples of these lands, those who have historically inhabited the Sierra Nevada and those who still live today about the great range: the many peoples of the Koyom:kʼawi (Konkow); the Mountain Maidu; the Nisenan; the Wašišiw ítdeh (Washoe); the Me-Wuk (Central and Southern Sierra Miwok); the Western Mono/Monache; the Eastern Mono/Monache; the Newe (Western Shoshone); the Tübatulabal; the Numu (Northern Paiute); and the Western Shoshone (Newe). May I always walk humbly on land that is yours. May my every step be one of thankfulness.

—RJN

How is it that two families ended up taking on so daft and perilous a journey, in a high-water year; a journey that gave us the chance to lose ourselves in the beauties of the High Sierra? Because of the dreaming of Lucy Blake, who holds the High Sierra within. Her life is all love and courage. Were it not for her conjuring this route, and her passionate urging of all of us to adventure, the trip would never have happened.

Part of the reason she has such dreams is her long history of hiking in the Sierra with her father, the late Bob Blake, to whom we all owe heartfelt gratitude. He, like his daughter, had the High Sierra memorized. Lucy and I did many outlandish hikes with him, and the memory is a deep joy. One of them was to 12,000 feet, when our daughter Gabriella was one year old.

Gabriella accustomed herself to sleeping on the ground and dancing over summits. She has been, and continues to be, far more than a daughter: a teacher, adventurer, and source of beautiful and challenging ideas. Blessings and thanks to her.

As to my own hiking in the Great Basin, the Colorado Plateau, and the tropics, I am indebted to my hiking companions of many decades, who were willing to join me on excursions that ranged from a weekend ramble to deep and crazy dives into canyons where the only certainties are transformative beauty and possible death. You know who you are. No one can ever take those journeys away from us. Thank you.

I have, over thirty years, had many mentors and compatriots in the world of books. At table with the Dante scholar and extraordinary friend Rachel Jacoff,

I have had the most far-ranging conversations about a wilderness of a different kind: the wilderness within books essential to life. With Andrea Wilson Nightingale I had years of musing that transformed how I thought about everything in the world; and made a new life possible.

One woman has played an extraordinary and unique role for all those thirty years: the blessed Elizabeth Dilly, whose mind is deft, open, improvisational, and honest. Every book I have written has had the benefit of her bemused insights, sharp corrections, and intuitive commentary. With her help and affection my work in language, over the decades, became for me a trustworthy joy.

No writer is without the company of fellow workers in this strange field. With the celebrated poet Robert Hass, I have had various rambles and long woolgathering exchanges about verse. He has done me many kindnesses, for which I am deeply thankful. My dear friend David Lee is one of the preeminent poets of the American West and of our country. He combines a capacious mind with a deep and raucous experience of life.

And no writer can live without a world-class bookstore nearby. Mine is Sundance Books, run by my generous and indispensable friend Christine Kelly.

In my home state of Nevada, my thanks to the deeply gifted musician and writer Robert Leonard Reid. Robert once compiled a book of essays on the Sierra Nevada which is still one of the definitive works of its kind.

To Mattias Lanas, the artist who with the most painstaking care created the drawings that accompany each pair of essays: thank you for the beautiful images, and for being so patient with our countless wild comments upon your evolving art.

To the anonymous donor who, out of the blue, mischievously offered to fund Mattias's work: we were touched and delighted by your faith in us.

Our editor at Cornell University Press, Kitty Liu, has been superb: intelligent, professional, unfailingly helpful. Her suggestions in every case made our book more complete, more evocative of our experience on the hike, and more accessible to the reader. And let me join Richard in thanks to Craig Childs, an exceptionally helpful and astute reviewer, and the anonymous reviewer who read our book with such close, thorough, and discerning attention.

And to Richard Nevle, Deborah Levoy, and their daughter Sophie: we have shared a miraculous land, and your company brought to our journey a special beauty and inconceivable joy. I simply do not know how I ever could have gotten so lucky as to have the three of you as my brave, dear, brilliant friends.

—Steven Nightingale

NOTES

PREFACE

ix *There is a way of beholding nature that is itself a form of prayer.* Ackerman 1992, xiv.

xi *to step out from behind our personas—whatever they might be: educators, activists, biologists, geologists, writers, farmers, ranchers, and bureaucrats* Williams 1994, 84.

GRANITE

12 *Granite is the geologic backbone of the Sierra Nevada. Granite* has a specific meaning as a geologic term, referring to intrusive igneous rocks having a high weight percent of silica (SiO_2) and a specific, limited range of proportions of the minerals quartz, plagioclase feldspar, and potassium feldspar (Le Bas and Streckeisen 1991). Here we use the term granite more expansively to refer to all *granitic* rocks, a category inclusive of granite as well as its slightly silica-poorer cousins tonalite and granodiorite, which are the dominant intrusive rock types found in the Sierra Nevada.

12 *secreting caustic acids and digesting minerals* The excretion of organic acids by lichens is but one of many ways these communal organisms contribute to the weathering of rocks through a variety of physical and chemical processes (Chen, Blume, and Beyer 2000).

12 *stone monuments would decompose* We invoke a thought experiment to accelerate time and imagine how lichen affects the weathering of rock. Indeed, the effects can be observed over the course of a few human generations. The deterioration of stone structures and monuments of world cultural heritage sites across the globe, induced by lichens and other biological agents, is a source of major concern for their preservation (X. Liu et al. 2020).

12 *granite is a product of life, a rock unique to Earth, made possible by photosynthesis* Rosing et al. (2006) make a compelling case for the role that photosynthetic microbes played in catalyzing the geological conditions on early Earth that were necessary for generating abundant volumes of granite. Grosch and Hazen (2015) describe how microbes that derive their metabolic energy directly from rock contributed to the hydration of the young Earth's basaltic crust, an important preconditioning that enables the partial melting of basalt and the generation of melts that can be compositionally modified during their ascent through continental crust to become granite.

12 *dense slabs of seafloor rock plunge into the Earth's scalding interior* Many texts provide overviews of the theory of plate tectonics and descriptions of the associated processes of subduction, partial melting, and magma genesis that lead to the production of granite. We have encountered errors in many books, including some geology textbooks, in explanations of the underlying physical and chemical mechanisms that drive these fundamental geologic processes. For clarity and accuracy, we recommend the lucidly written and beautifully illustrated *Understanding Earth* by Grotzinger and Jordan (2019), now a classic in its eighth edition.

13 *"The sun is but a morning star."* Last line of Conclusion in Thoreau 2006, 309.

13 *"As soon as you entered this world of forms, an escape ladder was put out for you."* Shah 2015, 80.

13 *"This world is not conclusion."* Dickinson 1951, 243.

OBSIDIAN

16 *obsidian craters just east of the range erupted in the last few millennia, some in recent centuries* We refer here to the rhyolite domes of the Mono Craters and the related Inyo Craters, both south of Mono Lake, California. A review of the geologic history of these striking volcanic features can be found in Sharp and Glazner 1997.

16 *making granite requires time enough for melt to cool slowly in the insulating warmth of earth's crust* The growth of crystals in magma chambers several miles below Earth's surface, like those that solidified to form the great Sierra Nevada batholith, is quite slow—on the order of a thousandth of a millimeter per year (Paterson and Tobisch 1992).

16 *can in fact be flaked into tools with edges that are many times sharper than a razor blade* Buck 1982; Marmelzat 1987.

17 *What stories did they tell, these hunters and their kin, on dark summer nights as they gazed upon the cradling arms of the Milky Way, of how the stone that took life and gave life came itself into life?* See Hodgson 2007 for an informative account of the myriad uses of obsidian by California's Native peoples.

18 *"Your body is like earth and your head the sky. Your bones are like mountains, rough and hard. Vegetation is your hair and trees are your limbs."* Shabistari 2007, 125.

ROOF PENDANTS

20 *They journeyed across the great Panthalassic Ocean, ancestor of the Pacific, ferried aboard a tectonic plate that slid eastward until it encountered western North America.* See Moore 2000, Hill 2006, and Meldahl 2011 for more thorough treatments of the geologic origins of the Sierra Nevada's roof pendants. These references all provide excellent overviews of the geologic history of the Sierra Nevada.

20 *For more than a hundred million years this plate, the Farallon Plate, pulled by its immense, dense mass, bent where it met the continent and descended into the mantle's scorching interior.* Tectonic plates composed of oceanic lithosphere (oceanic crust plus the rocky portion of the upper mantle), when they are sufficiently dense, sink into more ductile and more buoyant mantle material below. The density difference between the sinking plate and the mantle into which it descends is small, only about 1 percent, but this difference is enough to drive the movements of Earth's tectonic plates at speeds on the order of centimeters per year, which over hundreds of millions of years can open and close ocean basins.

20 *In the last few millions of years, the amalgam of deformed exotic rocks has risen miles into the sky, even as the range has been given line and shape and texture by glaciers and rivers.* The southern Sierra Nevada—i.e., the "High Sierra," where the High Sierra Trail is located—likely declined in stature throughout much of the early Cenozoic (around sixty-six to twenty-three million years ago) but subsequently began to rise (McPhillips and Brandon 2012). The Northern Sierra Nevada, by contrast, likely attained its present elevation by around fifty million years ago

(Chamberlain et al. 2012; Cassel et al. 2012; Henry et al. 2012; Cecil et al. 2006). See Meldahl 2011 for an overview of the Sierra's complex history of vertical movement.

20 *Once horizontal layers of seafloor sediment are now accordioned.* A stunning example of metamorphosed, intensely folded marine sediments can be found on the north side of the Kings River along State Route 180, just east of Boyden Cavern in the Sequoia National Forest.

20 *The delicate edifices of coral reefs have recrystallized into mosaics of scintillant calcite, revealed in Sierra caverns.* Stunning photographs of the parks' caves can be found in Despain 2003, which also describes the caves' fascinating human and natural history. Both Crystal Cave in Sequoia National Park and Boyden Cavern in the Sequoia National Forest provide relatively accessible ingress to the Sierra's mysterious subterranean beauty.

20 *Such mineral stains occasionally reveal deposits of dispersed gold, silver, tungsten, copper, and other valuable metals that formed when superheated, mineral-charged waters escaped from crystallizing granite and reacted with the seafloor remnants.* See Moore 2000 for a discussion of the formation of mineral deposits in the High Sierra.

20 *Such soils, in the austere climatic conditions of high elevation, nurture gardens with delicate wildflowers you will not find blossoming elsewhere in the Sierra* Soils that develop on most kinds of metamorphic rock found in the Sierra's roof pendants provide a more nurturing environment for plants than soils derived from granite. First, soils derived from metamorphic rock are more nutrient-rich than their granite-derived counterparts. Second, because metamorphic rocks decompose more readily than granite, weathering of them produces soils that tend to be deeper and therefore better at retaining moisture. Third, soils derived from most metamorphic rocks are also darker in color and therefore better at absorbing heat than those derived from granite. By contrast, soils that develop on marble, a metamorphic rock composed mostly of the mineral calcite, are quite limited in phosphorous, an essential plant nutrient. Some plants have adapted to the nutrient-poor conditions found in relatively uncommon patches of marble-derived soils in the Sierra. This has given rise to ecological islands inhabited by endemic species of flowering plants. See Wenk 2015 and the references therein for a more thorough discussion of these phenomena.

21 *"The sun, moon, and the stars, the sky, earth, and sea, in all their phenomena and elements; and all inanimate objects, as well as plants, animals, and men . . . belong to one great system of all-conscious and interrelated life, in which the degrees of relationship seemed to be determined largely, if not wholly, by the degrees of resemblance."* Introduction of Cushing 1991.

BROKENNESS

24 *it shatters like a beer bottle left too long in the freezer* See pp. 52–53 of Bill Green's *Water, Ice & Stone: Science and Memory on the Antarctic Lakes* for a dramatic account of water's unusual property of expansion as it nears its freezing point (Green 2008).

25 *Geologists have described whole families of joints cutting through the granites of the Sierra Nevada* See Moore 2000 and Glazner and Stock 2010 for overviews of the origin of fault and joint systems in the Sierra Nevada.

25 *Some joints formed soon after the granite crystallized from melt and mineral slushes in glowing wombs deep below the surface.* See, for example, Bergbauer and Martel 1999.

25 *Some joints are stretch marks, traces of breakage under tension.* See, for example, Lockwood and Moore 1979.

25 *Another family of joints, paralleling the San Andreas Fault* See Glazner and Stock 2010.

25 *And another family of joints formed as the Sierra ascended to the surface* See Martel 2017.

25 *Range of Light* On first gazing upon the Sierra Nevada from Pacheco Pass in 1868, John Muir famously wrote:

> From the eastern boundary of this vast golden flower-bed rose the mighty Sierra, miles in height, and so gloriously colored and so radiant, it seemed not clothed with light but wholly composed of it, like the wall of some celestial city. . . . Then it seemed to me that the Sierra should be called, not the Nevada or Snowy Range, but the Range of Light." (Muir 1912)

25 *it reveals itself for the first time in its hundred-million-year-old history* For simplicity, we refer to a single age for granitic rocks of the Sierra, yet the four-hundred-mile-long Sierra Nevada batholith comprises hundreds of individual granitic plutons emplaced between roughly 120 and 80 million years ago (Moore 2000). The much older metamorphic roof pendants of the Sierra predate these granitic rocks by hundreds of millions of years.

CLOUDS

30 *A cloud is a gathering of mist, trillions of droplets of water, each droplet the size of a corpuscle of blood.* The diameter of water droplets in clouds typically ranges from ten to fifty micrometers (Pruppacher and Klett 2010), slightly larger than the diameter of red blood cells in humans (about eight micrometers).

31 *Water contained within a modest cumulus cloud might weigh as much as few bison.* A hypothetical spherical cloud with a radius of 200 meters and a liquid water content of 0.2 grams per cubic meter has a water mass of 6,700 kilograms—that of about eight average-sized American bison.

31 *The water in a towering thunderhead might weigh as much as a herd of them, one million strong.* Cumulonimbus clouds have masses of water on the order of billions of kilograms, which translates, by mass, into millions of bison, assuming a modest cloud liquid water content of 0.2 grams per cubic meter.

31 *Freezing droplets of mist in the upper reaches of the cloud explode into glinting ice flecks.* See Saunders 2008 and Williams 1988 for reviews of the microphysical processes that occur during cloud electrification.

31 *A bolt of lightning contains a tiny fraction of this energy, but transformed and concentrated into electricity.* A typical lightning strike releases several gigajoules of energy (Williams 1988), enough to power an energy-efficient vehicle for several thousand miles. By contrast, the amount of energy required to lift the water vapor in a large thunderhead is on the order of several hundreds of thousands of gigajoules.

31 *hotter than the surface of the sun* The temperature of lightning has been estimated to be approximately twenty-four thousand degrees Kelvin (Uman 1964), more than four times hotter than the sun's surface, which is about 5,800 degrees Kelvin.

SNOW

36 *Crowns of thrumming molecules link to other crowns, millions upon millions arrayed in a latticed sheet, arranged like cells in a bee's honeycomb.* See Pruppacher and Kent 2010 for a more thorough discussion of ice structure and the forms of ice found in clouds.

36 *Sheets stack upon sheets to form an individual snowflake, which itself might contain more than ten billion billion molecules of water.* Individual snowflakes have masses of around a milligram (Szyrmer and Zawadzki 2010), and an individual water molecule has a mass of 2.992×10^{-23} grams. Simple division yields about 3×10^{19} (30 billion billion) water molecules for a 1 mg snowflake.

36 *A snowflake assembles itself within a cloud as molecules of water condense from vapor, perhaps around a grain of pollen or a speck of dust.* See Libbrecht 2005 for a technical review of the physics of snow formation. Libbrecht and Rasmussen's book *The Snowflake: Winter's Secret Beauty* provides a more accessible narrative of how snowflakes form and includes many stunning photographs of snowflakes (Libbrecht and Rasumssen 2003).

37 *The snowflake's form holds a story of wandering.* This process is discussed in more detail in Libbrecht and Rasmussen 2003.

37 *Wind-driven snow abrades trees clean down to the gold of heartwood.* The hardness of crystalline ice increases with decreasing temperature (Butkovich 1958), but even at temperatures just below freezing, ice's hardness exceeds that of soft woods like pine (Sydor, Pinkowski, and Jasí 2020).

37 *Trees are bannered by the passing of countless winter storms, which strip western, storm-fronting faces of trunks bare of branches.* We've observed this phenomenon in many of the Sierra's high elevation regions. You can see conspicuous examples of storm-flagged trees just off the road from Tioga Pass (Highway 120) and Carson Pass (Highway 89).

GLACIER

42 *Like all mountain glaciers, those of the Sierra began high up in the range where massing snow persisted in shadowed mountain cradles through summer.* See Ruddiman 2013 for an explanation of the process of glacial inception.

43 *the glaciers now in the Sierra emerged only a few centuries ago when California's climate turned cooler and wetter for several hundred years, many millennia after the passage of the last great ice age* See Moore 2000, Gillespie and Zehfuss 2004, Glazner and Stock 2010, and Moore and Moring 2013 for reviews of the glacial history of the Sierra Nevada. See Clark and Gillespie 1997 for a discussion of the most recent episode of glacial advance in the Sierra (known as the Matthes advance) during a cool period lasting from around 1450 to around 1850 CE (Graumlich 1993).

43 *Bubbles dispersed throughout the glaciers' mosaics of crystalline ice preserved tiny time capsules of trapped air, bearing witness to the increasing concentration of greenhouse gases in the atmosphere.* This statement applies generally to all glaciers, though the relatively warm conditions that prevail in the low-latitude alpine environments in which Sierran glaciers have developed (as compared to polar regions) are suboptimal for preserving continuous snow-accumulation records necessary for detailed reconstructions of climatic history (temperature and precipitation) and atmospheric greenhouse gas variations. Although ice cores extracted from Antarctic glaciers provide the gold standard for such reconstructions, it may be possible to extract some meaningful climate-related information from glaciers still remaining in the Sierra (Gillespie 2006).

43 *the ice attaining a mass so great it slowly collapsed under its weight, yielding to gravity in a slow, fluid cascade downslope* By definition a glacier is a body of ice that has grown so large that it begins to flow internally. Typically this begins to happen after a glacier has accumulated a thickness of about fifty meters.

43 *But it is the rock itself, polished to a mirror-smooth finish by ice-borne rock flour, that flashes so brightly in the sun.* This is always striking wherever once sees it in the Sierra. One of our favorite locations to observe this phenomenon is in the Tuolumne Meadows region of Yosemite National Park, where it can be seen on many of the glacially polished domes.

43 *The ice sprawled from icefields the size of metropolises* The largest of the Sierra's glaciers at the time of the last glacial maximum approximately twenty thousand years ago continued from Mount Lyell for a distance of almost fifty miles down the Grand Canyon of the Tuolumne River and on through the Hetch Hetchy Valley.

44 *cognitive scientist Gregory Bateson* These ideas are discussed in *Steps to an Ecology of Mind*, passim, and especially in Part V, "Epistemology and Ecology" in Bateson 1987.

45 *"If the doors of perception were cleansed, everything would appear . . . as it is, infinite."* From *The Marriage of Heaven and Hell* (Blake 1982, 39).

45 *"To the eyes of a man of imagination, nature is imagination itself."* From a letter to Revd. Dr. Trusler (Blake 1982, 702).

45 *"Man has no Body distinct from his soul; for that called Body is a portion of a Soul discerned by the five senses, the chief inlets of Soul in this age."* From *The Marriage of Heaven and Hell* (Blake 1982, 34).

45 "If a thing loves, it is infinite." From the annotations of Swedenborg (Blake 1982, 604).

RIVER

48 *Into this shallow sea, ancestral rivers unloaded their hauls of Sierran rock in such quantity that the seafloor sagged and sank under the accumulating weight.* Such features, known in geological parlance as forearc basins, are characteristic of zones of plate convergence and subduction. See Grotzinger and Jordan 2019.

48 *Remnants of the river-ferried and ocean-sifted sediments are stacked between the Sierra and the Coast Ranges in a bulging wedge of rock up to six miles thick.* See Bartow and Nilsen 1990.

48 *The volume of it might fill the Grand Canyon twenty-five times over.* This is a conservative estimate, based on an approximated volume of the sedimentary rocks of the Great Valley Sequence and a volume of about 4,200 km³ for the Grand Canyon.

49 *bona-fide river deposits now exposed in highway roadcuts* Eocene streams carried and deposited auriferous (gold-bearing) gravels derived from accreted metamorphosed terranes. These gravels accumulated in thick channel deposits, such as that preserved at Malakoff Diggins, that were later targeted by powerful jets of water blasted from the monitors of nineteenth-century hydraulic miners. See Hill 2006 for more discussion and a description of locations where you can see these deposits.

49 *a broad welt of mountains hundreds of miles wider than the present-day Sierra* Around eighty million years ago, the Farallon Plate may have begun to ride high beneath the western edge of North America (see references cited in Meldahl 2011). The reason for this is thought to relate to the possible existence of thickened, buoyant welt in the Farallon Plate that resisted subduction (Humphreys et al. 2003; L. Liu et al. 2010; Meldahl 2011). As the putatively welt-thickened plate was dragged beneath the western edge of the North American continental plate by the Farallon's dense, leading edge, it floated on—rather than sank into—the underlying mantle. Like a dog crawling under a rug, the welt pushed the region above it into a broad mountainous plateau dubbed the Nevadaplano (DeCelles 2004) based on its geographic resemblance to the Andean Altiplano.

49 *Rivers wandered the fat range through evergreen subtropical forests of magnolia, breadfruit, fig, palm, persimmon, and laurel* See MacGinitie 1941.

49 *soils weathered a deep brick red in the balmy and humid climate of a younger Sierra* See Hill (2006) for a description of the Eocene laterite soils exposed in many locations of the Sierra Nevada foothills.

49 *you can still trace the paths of a few of the ancestral rivers, preserved where steaming lava flows poured into their valleys* We refer here to formations like Table Mountain, visible from Highway 120 near Jamestown, California. This distinctive landform is, in effect, a cast of the mold of the ancestral Stanislaus River valley. The feature is composed of lava flows that poured into the valley and then later resisted erosion more effectively than the surrounding rocks. See also Hill 2006 and Glazner and Stock 2010.

49 *It is said that Heraclitus of Ephesus, a philosopher of Ancient Greece, once stated that we cannot step into the same river twice.* See Graham 2019.

50 *"Those that are worthy of life are of miracle, for life is a miracle, and death, harmless as a bee, except to those who run."* Letter to Susan Gilbert Dickinson, September 1864 (Dickinson 1958, 186).

FOREST

54 *As glaciers retreated, species of pine and cedar and fir and hemlocks marched their way up into the high country, trailing the hems of melting glaciers.* Millar and Woolfenden 1999.

54 *Eleven thousand years ago, at the end of Earth's most recent glaciation, glaciers sprawled across the range like sleeping cats. Forests grew at the Sierra's edges, at much lower elevations than they do today.* Millar and Woolfenden 1999; Gillespie and Zehfuss 2004.

54 *It's possible that some of the oldest sequoia monarchs now standing in the Sierra are members of only the second generation to have ever lived there.* The oldest known giant sequoia is almost 3,300 years old (Stephenson 2000) and sprouted a little more than a millennium after giant sequoias began to inhabit the groves that they now occupy in the Sierra (Millar and Woolfenden 1999).

55 *These orbital gyrations, pulsing over periods of tens of thousands of years, vary the intensity of sunlight striking Earth over time.* See Ruddiman 2013 and Grotzinger and Jordan 2019.

55 *Recent warming in the range, brought on by increasing average global temperature caused by greenhouse gas emissions from human activities, has pushed seedlings of several of the range's iconic conifer species—the mountain hemlock, the red fir, the western white pine—to start putting down roots at elevations more than a hundred meters higher than where they did a century ago.* See Wright, Nguyen, and Anderson 2016.

55 *In 2015, when California was in the midst of a brutal, six-year drought, trees of the lower elevations of the Sierra Nevada—incense cedar and several species of pine, fir, and oak—were beginning to die en masse, particularly in the range's warmer southern regions.* See Fettig et al. 2019 and Goulden and Bales 2019.

55 *By 2016, many old sequoia giants in groves near our trailhead had begun to shed foliage high up in their canopies, hundreds of feet above ground, in an apparent attempt to cope with ongoing water stress.* See also Walker 2016.

55 *As of this writing in 2020, more than 147 million trees have perished in the Sierra Nevada as the result of the drought* Goulden and Bales 2019.

57 *"When much in the woods as a little girl, I was told that the snake would bite me, that I might pick a poisonous flower, or goblins kidnap me, but I went along and met no one but angels."* Letter to Thomas Higginson, August 1862 (Dickinson 1958, 178).

57 *"I was thinking today—as I noticed, that the 'Supernatural' was only the natural, disclosed."* Letter to Thomas Higginson, February 1863 (Dickinson 1958, 182).

FIRE

62 *Fire quite literally prepares the ground for the next generation* See Hartesveldt and Harvey 1967.

63 *Indigenous peoples used fire in the Sierra's mid-elevation forests as one tool in a suite of horticultural technologies to tend to the wild* See Anderson 2013.

63 *produced a varied mosaic of forest habitat* McKelvey et al. 1996; Safford and Stevens 2017; van Wagtendonk et al. 2018.

63 *It was the kind of forest in which the Sierra's rare great gray owl could hide among shady stands of trees and search adjacent moonlit meadows for sustenance. It was the kind of forest in which now threatened animals like the black-backed woodpecker, the California spotted owl, and the ferocious Pacific fisher thrived.* Bond et al. 2009; Hanson 2013; Hanson and Odion 2016; Jones et al. 2016; Campos et al. 2019; Tingley et al. 2020; White et al. 2019.

63 *Policies of fire suppression enacted in the late nineteenth and early twentieth centuries* One of the most lucid and invigorating accounts of the political history of fire suppression in the United States can be found in Timothy Egan's marvelously written book *The Big Burn: Teddy Roosevelt and the Fire that Saved America* (Egan 2010).

63 *Today, many of the Sierra's forested landscapes captured in historical photographs are almost unrecognizable* See Charles Gruell's collection of photographs in *Fire in Sierra Nevada Forests: A Photographic Interpretation of Ecological Change Since 1849* (Gruell 2001).

64 *the Sierra Nevada's forests store among the highest levels of carbon on a per area basis of any forest in the continental United States* See the dataset of above-ground carbon density produced by Spawn and Gibbs 2010.

64 *Too little moisture, and trees can't marshal flows of sap to defend against onslaughts of bark beetles* See Bentz et al. 2010.

64 *As California's climate warms, less snow falls and less snow lingers on through spring to moisten the heart of the range's conifer forests.* See Rauscher et al. 2008 and Lute, Abatzogolou, and Hegewisch 2015.

64 *Fires are burning hotter, lasting longer, consuming larger areas* See Jones et al. 2016 and Kelsey 2019.

64 *burning more frequently higher up in the range—in the cool, moist, previously fire-resistant lodgepole pine forests—than at any time in recorded history* See Schwartz et al. 2015.

64 *Some ecologists worry that trees won't recover in the range's mid-elevations once fire and damage by bark-beetles clears them out. They worry that mid-elevations of the range could be in the midst of a wholesale transition from forest to chaparral. Others think we might be able to work our way back toward a healthy forest mosaic, using prescribed burns that whittle away the backlog of accumulated fuel.* See Young et al. 2019, Rother et al. 2019, Wood and Jones 2019, and Stephens et al. 2020.

66 *"Truth imposes upon us . . . evident"* Shah 2017, 113.

67 *"When the house burns down, save the nails."* Merwin 1973, 18.

BIGHORN

72 *Considered a genetically distinct subspecies of the bighorn sheep known across the montane regions of the North American West* See U.S. Fish and Wildlife Service 2007.

72 *The horns are composed of a spongy shock-absorbing core of bone sheathed in flexible, spring-like keratin . . . One can roughly estimate a ram's age by the number of deep grooves demarcating the horn's annual growth rings.* See Drake et al. 2016 and Ballard 2014.

72 *horns of a mature ram might weigh thirty pounds* See Ballard 2014.

73 *animals are able to squeeze blood into vessels that supply the brain, producing a kind of cranial bubble wrap* See Myer et al. 2014.

73 *The defeated might still have a chance, but only if they can manage to employ more surreptitious means to arrange furtive couplings.* See Hogg 1984.

73 *For millennia the Sierra bighorn thrived despite these difficulties, until the nineteenth century at least, when the introduction of domestic sheep, which brought new diseases and competition for forage, and increased hunting began to winnow the population of Sierra bighorn.* See U.S. Fish and Wildlife Service 2007.

73 *A few days before giving birth, an expectant ewe will leave her herd in search of refuge in some remote haunt of the range, perhaps the very site of her own emergence into the world.* See Ballard 2014.

73 *For this sense of safety, the ewe treads, metaphorically, on an edge, trading prospect for protection, forgoing access to the best quality forage (and the nutritious milk it would have supplied)* Lactating female bighorns seek habitat near "escape terrain" that affords high visibility and where the chances of encountering mountain lions is low (Forshee 2018).

73 *Elders are vital to lambs' survival.* See Ballard 2014.

74 *spiraling perilously close to the edge of what ecologists call an extinction vortex* See Johnson 2010.

74 *Sierra bighorn had become so few in number that the accumulating effects of inbreeding, compounded by one or two bad years—be it in the form of increased predation, disease outbreak, a particularly brutal winter, or a drought resulting in low forage production—threatened to push the Sierra bighorn past the edge of existence, to become forever gone.* See Johnson 2010 and U.S. Fish and Wildlife Service 2007.

74 *The bighorn's perilous situation catalyzed an aggressive recovery effort* See U.S. Fish and Wildlife Service 2007. We also recommend a breathtaking mini-documentary from the Yosemite Nature Notes series on bighorn sheep reintroduction to the Cathedral Range of Yosemite National Park (National Park Service 2015).

74 *Part of the recovery effort also involved the highly controversial culling of mountain lions in areas of the range in which predation by lions had winnowed down numbers of reintroduced herds.* Rosen 2017.

74 *The population of Sierra bighorn has responded to this ongoing endeavor* See U.S. Fish and Wildlife Service 2007.

75 *"If a man has not discovered something he will die for, he isn't fit to live."* King 1965.

76 *"A solved problem is as useful to us as a broken sword on a battlefield."* Shah 1989, 142.

76 *"Counterfeiters exist because there is such a thing as real gold."* Shah 2015, 77.

76 *"He who has made a door and a lock has also made a key."* Shah 2015, 117.

ASPEN

80 *"There is another world,"* wrote the poet Paul Éluard, *"and it is this one."* This quote was attributed to the French poet Paul Éluard by Heather King (King 2007), as it has been in numerous sources. Yet after an extensive search we have not been able to identify the original source. We defer here to McKenzie Wark's commentary (Wark 2014) on the origin of this statement, which for now still remains elusive.

81 *Each individual tree might live for a century or so, until fire or disease or old age finally take its life, to leave a sunny opening where shoots may spring from the mother root below.* See DeByle and Winokur 1985 and Mitton and Grant 1996.

81 *In spring you can distinguish each aspen colony* See DeByle and Winokur 1985.

81 *they begin a nearly month-long process of metamorphosis* See Keskitalo et al. 2005.

81 *The turning of aspen leaves is an event of astronomical proportions.* According to Keskitalo et al. (2005), individual aspen leaves have about thirty million cells, and each of those cells contains around forty chloroplasts. Assuming that the number of leaves on typical aspen trees ranges from ten thousand to one million, the typical number of chloroplasts in an aspen might range on the order of 10–100 trillion chloroplasts per tree. Most estimates of the number of stars in our galaxy are on the order of 100 billion.

81 *a conifer's photosynthetic machinery can rev up for a few hours to take advantage of the brief, intense sunlight* See Kelly and Goulden 2016.

81 *the tree's thin, powdery-white layer of outer bark lies a pale green sheath of tissue that enables the tree to photosynthesize through the cold days of winter* See Pearson and Lawrence 1958.

PAINTBRUSH

86 *Species of* Castilleja *occur throughout the Sierra* A few of our favorite references for Sierra flower identification are those by Botti and Sydoriak 2001, Wiese 2001, Laws 2007, and Wenk 2015.

86 *the root of the paintbrush might more accurately be described as a haustorium* See Yoshida et al. 2016.

86 *Roots of most plants, perhaps following some sensory capacity akin to our animal sense of smell* See Chamovitz 2017.

87 *they need nutrients from their hosts* In addition to drawing water and nutrients from their hosts, at least one member of the *Castilleja* genus (*Castilleja miniata*) that associates with a particular species of lupine may experience less herbivory and produce more seeds than those parasitizing different hosts (Adler 2002).

87 *The paintbrushes, by drawing from host plants that might otherwise dominate the local floral neighborhood, diminish their hosts' tendency to overwhelm it and in so doing enable a more diverse variety of flowering species to flourish.* See Phoenix and Press 2005 and Reed 2012.

88 *releasing an abundance of stored nourishment to the soil* See Phoenix and Press 2005 and Press 2016.

WHITEBARK AND NUTCRACKER

94 *Clark's Nutcracker* The Clark's nutcracker is named for William Clark. The wildlife photographer Darren Cook (in a personal communication) proposed that the bird's name might be changed to honor York, an African American man who contributed indispensably to the Lewis and Clark expedition and who was enslaved by Clark. York's nutcracker has a rather nice ring to it, we think.

95 *"made for each other,"* RJN's essay on the cooperative partnership between the whitebark pine and the nutcracker was inspired by Ronald M. Lanner's beautifully written and informative account of the mutualism between pines with wingless seeds and their avian caretakers in *Made for Each Other: A Symbiosis of Birds and Pines* and many references therein (Lanner 1996), as well as by many happy encounters with both species in the Sierra.

96 *"The candle burned the moth, but soon it will vanish in its own fat."* Shah 1989, 85.

96 *"The sailor cannot see the North, but knows the needle can."* Letter to Thomas Higginson, June 1862 (Dickinson 1958, 172).

PILEATED WOODPECKER

100 *Anatomy helps.* For a more detailed description of the intricate anatomy that enables woodpeckers to withstand high impact blows, see Shunk 2016.

100 *The bird does not seem to mind the labor, for an individual pileated woodpecker will roost in numerous sites during the course of a few months, and monogamous pairs of pileated woodpeckers typically excavate a new nest cavity each year.* See Aubry and Raley 2002.

101 *All of this industrious labor has profound effects on our forest.* See Aubry and Raley 2002 for a more thorough treatment of how the pileated woodpecker serves as a "keystone habitat modifier" in forests.

101 *watch for the hulking old snags of trees* Pileated woodpeckers have been shown to have a preference for excavating their nests in "hard snags"–i.e., trees that have areas of soft, decaying wood (Harris 1980). See also Bunnell et al. 2002.

BELDING'S GROUND SQUIRREL

104 *Belding's ground squirrel pups tussling and tumbling* Observing young Belding's ground squirrel pups as they play is among the many joys of spending summer afternoons in the Sierra's high meadows. Marks et al. 2017 have documented extensive play behavior (including wrestling, boxing, tackling, and chasing) among Belding's pups and have shown that such behavior enhances the young squirrels' capacity to negotiate novel and stressful situations.

104 *The squirrels must consume a year's worth of calories in the span of a few green months* Prior to hibernation, 40–50 percent of the body weight of a Belding's ground squirrel is fat; about half of this fat remains when the animals emerge from their dens in spring (Morton and Sherman 1978).

104 *On sighting a raptor, a Belding's hurries for cover as it chirps out a high-pitched alarm call.* Belding's ground squirrels possess a kind of language. Many studies have shown that variations in bark patterns signal information about the imminence and location (aerial or ground) of predatory threats (Sherman 1977; Robinson 1981; Sherman 1985; McCowan and Hooper 2002).

104 *On seeing a predator approach on foot, a female Belding's will sound an alarm to alert her kin nearby.* Although male Belding's ground squirrels also whistle alarm calls, females do so more often, particularly in the presence of kin. See Sherman 1977, 1980, and 1985; and Shields 1980.

104 *Cold and starvation kill many.* See Morton and Sherman 1978.

105 *each mature female comes into estrus for only a few hours on a single day* To be more precise, females are sexually receptive for only about five hours on a single afternoon of a single day, and in that time may mate with up to five males (Hanken and Sherman 1981).

105 *Litters of five or so pups, often sired by several fathers, arrive about a month later.* See Hanken and Sherman 1981.

105 *a cozy, underground nest fashioned from soft roots and grass near the nesting burrows of female relatives* See Whitaker 1980.

105 *bonds of kinship with furry kisses* In the "kissing" behavior exhibited by Belding's ground squirrels, the animals are sniffing secretions from oral glands that allow them to identify relatives (Mateo 2003, 2017, 2020).

105 *guard their young against predation, infanticide, and even cannibalism* Female Belding's ground squirrels live in close proximity with other female relatives. They form highly cooperative social units who come to one another's defense and band together to chase off trespassers (Sherman 1981). One threat that kinship groups cannot defend against however is climate change. A study by Moritz et al. (2008) showed that the range of Belding's ground squirrel populations has contracted into the higher elevations of their historical range in the Sierra during the last century.

MOUNTAIN CHICKADEE

108 *Using sophisticated acoustic analyses, observant biologists have learned that the songs of mountain chickadees at higher elevations are different—in the timing and frequency of their notes—from the songs of their kin dwelling lower down.* See Branch and Pravosudov 2015 and Kozlovsky, Branch, and Pravosudov 2015.

108 *In addition, the high elevation mountain chickadee's hippocampus—a region of the brain associated with spatial memory—is larger and more neuron-dense than that of its lowland relative, giving them a superior ability to find cached stores of seed* See Freas et al. 2012.

108 *The birds' body temperatures cool by several degrees, so that they might conserve energy* See Cooper and Gessaman 2005.

MOUNTAIN YELLOW-LEGGED FROG

114 *you might notice a faint scent redolent of garlic* See Stebbins 2003.

114 *Rana sierrae dwells in the Sierra north of Mather Pass and the Monarch Divide; whereas her sister species, the longer legged Rana mucosa, inhabits the range to the south—and a few pocket-sized refuges in California's Transverse and Peninsular Ranges.* See Vredenburg et al. 2007.

114 *A century ago, wanderers of the High Sierra encountered mountain yellow-legged frogs in such plentitude* See Grinnell and Storer 1924 and Brown et al. 2014. See also Joseph Belli's moving essay on this subject (Belli 2018).

115 *They might overwinter two, maybe three more years before metamorphosing into full-grown frogs.* See Brown et al. 2014.

115 *Yet we took it upon ourselves, beginning in the late 19th century, to enable various species of trout to circumvent the redoubtable topographic barriers honed by glaciers, undoing the patient work of millennia in the matter of decades.* See Brown et al. 2014.

115 *Upon their arrival, trout—as predators with a penchant for eating anything they can wrap their lips around—began unraveling the lakes' delicate aquatic ecology.* See Knapp 1996.

116 *Knock-on effects rippled across the aquatic food web* See Schindler, Knapp, and Leavitt 2001.

116 *On land, garter snakes, who rely on the frogs as a choice dietary staple, began to decline.* See Jennings, Bradford, and Johnson 1992; and Knapp 2005.

116 *And the gray-crowned rosy-finch—a handsome mountaineer of a bird who haunts the Sierra's highest peaks—suffered as trout emptied lakes' larders.* See Epanchin, Knapp, and Lawler 2010.

116 *the disease known as chytridomycosis, or chytrid, a fungal infection that invades frogs' skin and kills by disrupting their ability to absorb nutrients, release toxins, and breathe, eventually leading to catastrophic organ failure and cardiac arrest* See Berger et al. 2016.

116 *Chytrid is a global pandemic that has reduced populations of more than 500 individual amphibian species, with 90 of those species likely extinct.* See Wake and Vredenburg 2008 and Scheele et al. 2019.

116 *Sierra mountain yellow-legged frogs have disappeared from more than 90% of their historical range* See Vredenburg et al. 2007; and Brown et al. 2014.

116 *Yet the mountain yellow-legged frogs' survival could not be more salient as we witness the catastrophic decline of populations of wild beings and the wholesale disappearance of species across the globe, with the loss being particularly acute in freshwater aquatic habitats.* See WWF 2020.

117 *In one study conducted in several lakes in Kings Canyon National Park and the adjacent John Muir Wilderness, the density of frog populations increased twelve- to forty-fold within a few years of fish removal, and from these recovering populations, frogs began dispersing to surrounding lakes.* See Knapp, Boiano, and Vredenburg 2007.

117 *Some mountain yellow-legged frog populations have shown signs of evolving a kind of fragile resistance.* See Woodhams et al. 2007; and Knapp et al. 2016.

117 *Meanwhile a few devoted groups of researchers endeavor to understand how to help frogs combat chytrid and tune strategies for conserving amphibian habitat, reintroducing healthy, lab-incubated, chytrid-resistant mountain yellow-legged frogs to areas of their ancestral range where they might thrive once again.* See Franz 2016.

118 *"From the Great Buddha's . . . comes gliding out."* Issa 1979, 157.

118 *"Smiling serenely . . . A little stinkworm."* Issa 1979, 88.

WESTERN TANAGER

122 *There is a German word,* zugunruhe, *which means a migratory restlessness* As described by Heinrich (2015), this term was coined by the German ornithologist, Gustav Kramer.

122 *They sing with questioning phrases—cher'-we?, chee'-we?, chir'-ru?, zee'-wer?* See Grinnell and Storer 1924.

122 *Many have described the tanager's behavior as subdued, even sluggish.* See Grinnell and Storer 1924 and Hudon 2020.

122 *Their faces are dipped in an incandescent blush of red-orange, which the birds acquire from rhodoxanthin—a pigment possibly obtained from their meals of insects, who themselves extract the compound from meals of conifer needles.* See Hudon 1991.

122 *Or perhaps they have evolved such vivid patterns of coloration simply because female western tanagers find it irresistibly sexy.* See Prum 2018.

123 *She lays perhaps four eggs, each about the size of a small grape* See Hudon 2020.

123 *The parents feed their young with insects gleaned from bark or branches or snatched adroitly from the air while on the wing—even dragonflies, which they will soften up in their capable beaks before feeding them, head first, to their gaping-mouthed babies.* See Hudon 2020.

123 *While tanagers are out foraging, this so-called nest parasite will seize upon the parents' momentary absence, and in secret she will lay a speckled egg among the unhatched brood.* See Fischer, Prather, and Cruz 2002.

123 *Each western tanager may make the annual journey to the Sierra Nevada and back again to its wintering grounds perhaps eight times during the course of its fleeting life.* See Hudon 2020.

125 *"unself yourself."* Sanai 1974, 36.

SIERRA NEVADA PARNASSIAN

128 *Devotees of the Sierra's butterfly fauna have found that more than 150 species inhabit the range* See Shapiro 1996.

128 *a male perched around a mud puddle, licking salt—which he may give as a love-offering to his mate, if he is lucky enough find one* Puddling behavior in the Sierra Nevada parnassian has not been reported in the literature; however, RJN observed this phenomenon in the Gaylor Lakes Basin of Yosemite National Park in August of 2016 with Ryan Carlton, a ranger who works seasonally in the Toulumne Meadows area.

128 *Or you might spy one floating up a steep talus slope to a rocky ridgetop, then fall like a leaf over a cliff on its other side.* The butterfly researcher Sean Schoville, a professor of entomology at the University of Wisconsin, Madison, finds this behavior to be one of the Sierra Nevada parnassian's most endearing. The behavior may be related to hill-topping, which males do in order to rendezvous with potential mates. RJN observed this phenomenon with Schoville in August 2019 after following a parnassian up a talus slope. The butterfly, after reaching the crest of the range, drifted through a narrow pass and preceded to cliff-dive over a precipitous edge into an abyss of space. One wonders, on all accounts, whether the butterflies might just be having fun.

128 *As the parnassian caterpillars gorge on their leafy diets, they accumulate a bitter organic compound called sarmentosin* This phenomenon has been observed in *Parnassius phoebus*, a close relative of the Sierra Nevada parnassian (Nishida and Rothschild 1995).

128 *a chemical relative of cyanide—which is produced in the plant kingdom uniquely by the stonecrop genus, and perhaps too by the crafty parnassian larvae themselves* See Nishida and Rothschild 1995 and Bjarnholt et al. 2012.

129 *As if poison were not enough, the young parnassian possesses a defense organ known as an osmeterium, which looks something like a fleshy snake's tongue. When threatened, our wee hero extends its osmeterium, simultaneously releasing a foul odor, the combination of which might be enough to the scare the hell out of most would be attackers.* See Matthews and Matthews 2010.

129 *Yet the caterpillars feed in the full light of day, when their warning-light speckles alone might dissuade predation most effectively.* See Nishida and Rothschild 1995.

129 *So as autumn approaches they must descend into a second hibernation* See James and Nunnallee 2011.

129 *Such striking designs, just as with the bright rows of yellow stipples of the Sierra Nevada parnassian's larvae, warn predators they had better think twice, lest they get a bitter mouthful of poison.* See Nishida and Rothschild 1995.

129 *They see beyond our vision into the ultraviolet range of the electromagnetic spectrum, sensing arrangements of petal coloration and geometric patterns imperceptible to our eyes.* Many pollinating insects, including at least one member of the *Parnassius* genus of butterflies, have the capacity to see into the ultraviolet range of the electromagnetic spectrum (Awata et al. 2010; Matsushita et al. 2012). Matsushita et al. 2012 hypothesize that the parnassian's eye, due to its unusual sensitivity to a broad spectrum of color relative to other butterfly species, has evolved to optimize for "extreme colour discrimination" rather than "acute spatial and motion vision."

129 *With their black-and-white striped antennae, they smell and taste* The Sierra Nevada parnassian's striped antennae readily distinguish it from the Clodius parnassian (*Parnassius clodius*), which also lives in the High Sierra but possesses antennae that are solid black.

130 *The Sierra Nevada parnassians might fly for the span of only a week* This estimate is based on a study by Scott (1974) of the *Parnassius phoebus* butterfly, which is in the same genus as the Sierra Nevada parnassian.

130 *"There is nothing one man will not do to another."* Forche 1982, 22.

WOLF LICHEN

134 *For lichens are a partnership of organisms—a fungus and a photosynthetic consort* See Spribille et al. 2016.

134 *In the wolf lichen partnership, yeast likely contributes by making vulpinic acid* See Spribille et al. 2016.

134 *the toxic, yellow-green compound that gives the lichen its ominous hue, provides a natural sunscreen, and shields it from herbivory by insects and mammals* See Slansky 1979; Stephenson and Rundel 1979; and Phinney et al. 2019.

134 *Even hummingbirds, who fancy lichens as a decorative camouflage on their demitasse-sized nests, don't find wolf lichen to their liking.* This is true insofar as we've observed in the Sierra Nevada. Surprisingly, little scholarship exists on the lichen composition of birds' nests, but one published analysis suggests that hummingbirds preferentially select foliose lichens (rather than fruticose types like wolf lichen) for nestbuilding purposes (McCormac and Showman 2009).

134 *In Scandinavia, the Sámi people used the lichen to poison wolves and foxes* See Svanberg and Ståhlberg 2017.

135 *Native peoples of western North America used preparations of wolf lichen for poisoning arrowheads, for treating various maladies of the skin and stomach, and for dyeing porcupine quills and yarns woven into vibrant basketry and textiles.* See Turnbaugh and Turnbaugh 1986; Svanberg and Ståhlberg 2017; and Crawford 2019.

135 *The Tlingit of Alaska have used wolf-lichen to dye yarns a pale, anemone-green* See Samuel 1982; and Turnbaugh and Turnbaugh 1986.

135 *healing potential of wolf lichen, in particular its superpowers in combatting cancer, meta-bolic diseases, and an antibiotic-resistant strain of bacteria, Staphylococcus aureus* See Shrestha et al. 2016; Kılıç, Aras, and Cansaran-Duman 2018; and Yi et al. 2019.

135 *As they capture nutrients from the atmosphere, they do so indiscriminately, absorbing what-ever airborne pollutants happen to fall upon them too. Sierra wolf lichens are bathed in a slew of wind-blown pesticides and pollutants produced by the incessant burning of fossil fuels.* See Jovan and McCune 2006; Jovan and Carlberg 2007; Mast, Alvarez, and Zaugg 2012; and Bermejo-Orduna et al. 2014.

135 *even as less pollution-tolerant relatives of the wolf lichen have likely declined in the range* See Fenn et al. 2003 and McCune et al. 2007.

REFERENCES

Ackerman, Diane. 1992. *The Moon by Whale Light: And Other Adventures Among Bats, Penguins, Crocodilians, and Whales*. New York: Vintage Books.

Addiss, Stephen. 2012. *The Art of Haiku: Its History Through Form and Painting*. Boston: Shambhala Publications.

Adler, Lynn S. 2002. "Host Effects on Herbivory and Pollination in a Hemiparasitic Plant." *Ecology* 83 (10): 2700–2710. https://doi.org/10.1890/0012-9658(2002)083[2700:HEOHAP]2.0.CO;2.

Anderson, M. Kat. 2005. *Tending the Wild: Native American Knowledge and the Management of California's Natural Resources*. Berkeley: University of California Press.

Aubry, Keith B, and Catherine M. Raley. 2002. *The Pileated Woodpecker as a Keystone Habitat Modifier in the Pacific Northwest. USDA Forest Service General Technical Report PSW-GTR-181.* https://www.fs.fed.us/psw/publications/documents/gtr-181/023_AubryRaley.pdf.

Awata, Hiroko, Atsuko Matsushita, Motohiro Wakakuwa, and Kentaro Arikawa. 2010. "Eyes with Basic Dorsal and Specific Ventral Regions in the Glacial Apollo, Parnassius Glacialis (Papilionidae)." *Journal of Experimental Biology* 213 (23): 4023–29. https://doi.org/10.1242/jeb.048678.

Ball, Philip. 1999. *The Self-Made Tapestry: Pattern Formation in Nature*. Oxford: Oxford University Press.

———. 2009. *Flow: Nature's Patterns, a Tapestry in Three Parts*. Oxford: Oxford University Press.

Ballard, Jack. 2014. *Falcon Pocket Guide: Bighorn Sheep*. Lanham, MD: Rowman & Littlefield.

Bartow, J. Allan, and Tor H. Nilsen. 1990. "Review of the Great Valley Sequence, Eastern Diablo Range and Northern San Joaquin Valley, Central California. U.S. Geological Survey Open-File Report 90-226." In *Structure, Stratigraphy and Hydrocarbon Occurrences of the San Joaquin Basin, California*. Society of Economic Paleontologists and Mineralogists, Pacific Section, Guidebook 65, edited by J. G. Kuespert and S. A. Reid, 253–65. Bakersfield, CA: Pacific Sections of the Society of Economic Paleontologists and Mineralogists and the American Association of Petroleum Geologists.

Bas, M. J. Le, and A. L. Streckeisen. 1991. "The IUGS Systematics of Igneous Rocks." *Journal of the Geological Society* 148 (5): 825–33. https://doi.org/10.1144/gsjgs.148.5.0825.

Bateson, Gregory. 1987. *Steps to an Ecology of Mind*. Northvale: Jason Aronson Inc.

Belli, Joseph. 2018. "After the Mountain Yellow-Legged Frog Disappeared." *High Country News*, August 6, 2018. https://www.hcn.org/issues/50.13/wildlife-after-the-mountain-yellow-legged-frog-disappeared.

Bentz, Barbara J., Jacques Régnière, Christopher J Fettig, E. Matthew Hansen, Jane L. Hayes, Jeffrey A. Hicke, Rick G. Kelsey, Jose F. Negrón, and Steven J. Seybold. 2010. "Climate Change and Bark Beetles of the Western United States and Canada: Direct and Indirect Effects." *BioScience* 60 (8): 602–13. https://doi.org/10.1525/bio.2010.60.8.6.

Bergbauer, Stephan, and Stephen J Martel. 1999. "Formation of Joints in Cooling Plutons." *Journal of Structural Geology* 21 (7): 821–35. https://doi.org/10.1016/S0191-8141(99)00082-6.

Berger, Lee, Alexandra A. Roberts, Jamie Voyles, Joyce E. Longcore, Kris A. Murray, and Lee F. Skerratt. 2016. "History and Recent Progress on Chytridiomycosis in Amphibians." *Fungal Ecology* 19 (February): 89–99. https://doi.org/10.1016/j.funeco.2015.09.007.

Bermejo-Orduna, R., J. R. McBride, K. Shiraishi, D. Elustondo, E. Lasheras, and J. M. Santamaría. 2014. "Biomonitoring of Traffic-Related Nitrogen Pollution Using Letharia Vulpina (L.) Hue in the Sierra Nevada, California." *Science of the Total Environment* 490 (August): 205–12. https://doi.org/10.1016/j.scitotenv.2014.04.119.

Bjarnholt, Nanna, Miroslaw Nakonieczny, Andrzej Kedziorski, Diane M. Debinski, Stephen F. Matter, Carl Erik Olsen, and Mika Zagrobelny. 2012. "Occurrence of Sarmentosin and Other Hydroxynitrile Glucosides in Parnassius (Papilionidae) Butterflies and Their Food Plants." *Journal of Chemical Ecology* 38 (5): 525–37. https://doi.org/10.1007/s10886-012-0114-x.

Blake, William. 1982. *The Complete Poetry and Prose of William Blake*. Edited by David Erdman. New York: Anchor.

Bond, Monica L., Derek E. Lee, Rodney B. Siegel, and James P. Ward. 2009. "Habitat Use and Selection by California Spotted Owls in a Postfire Landscape." *Journal of Wildlife Management* 73 (7): 1116–24. https://doi.org/10.2193/2008-248.

Botti, Stephen J., and Walter Sydoriak. 2001. *An Illustrated Flora of Yosemite National Park*. El Portal, CA: Yosemite Association/Heyday Books.

Branch, C. L., and V. V. Pravosudov. 2015. "Mountain Chickadees from Different Elevations Sing Different Songs: Acoustic Adaptation, Temporal Drift or Signal of Local Adaptation?" *Royal Society Open Science* 2 (4): 150019. https://doi.org/10.1098/rsos.150019.

Brehm, John, ed. 2017. *The Poetry of Impermanence, Mindfulness, and Joy*. Somerville: Wisdom Press.

Brown, Cathy, Marc Hayes, Gregory Green, and Diane MacFarlane. 2014. *Mountain Yellow-Legged Frog Conservation Assessment for the Sierra Nevada Mountains of California, USA—A Collaborative Interagency Project*. USDA Technical Report RS-TP-038. https://doi.org/10.13140/ 2.1.4787.5204

Buck, B. A. 1982. "Ancient Technology in Contemporary Surgery." *Western Journal of Medicine* 136 (3): 265–69.

Bunnell, Fred L, Isabelle Houde, Barb Johnston, and Elke Wind. 2002. *How Dead Trees Sustain Live Organisms in Western Forests*. USDA Forest Service Gen. Tech. Rep. https://www.fs.fed.us/psw/publications/documents/gtr-181/025_BunnellHoude.pdf.

Butkovich, T. R. 1958. "Hardness of Single Ice Crystals." *American Mineralogist* 43 (January-February): 48–57.

Campos, Brent R., Quresh S. Latif, Ryan D. Burnett, and Victoria A. Saab. 2019. "Predictive Habitat Suitability Models for Nesting Woodpeckers Following Wildfire in the Sierra Nevada and Southern Cascades of California." *Condor* 122 (1): 1–27. https://doi.org/10.1093/condor/duz062.

Cassel, E. J., S. A. Graham, C. P. Chamberlain, and C. D. Henry. 2012. "Early Cenozoic Topography, Morphology, and Tectonics of the Northern Sierra Nevada and Western Basin and Range." *Geosphere* 8 (2): 229–49. https://doi.org/10.1130/GES00671.1.

Cecil, M. R., M. N. Ducea, P. W. Reiners, and C. G. Chase. 2006. "Cenozoic Exhumation of the Northern Sierra Nevada, California, from (U-Th)/He Thermochronology." *Geological Society of America Bulletin* 118 (11–12): 1481–88. https://doi.org/10.1130/B25876.1.

Chamberlain, C. P., H. T. Mix, A. Mulch, M. T. Hren, M. L. Kent-Corson, S. J. Davis, T. W. Horton, and S. A. Graham. 2012. "The Cenozoic Climatic and Topographic Evolution of the Western North American Cordillera." *American Journal of Science* 312 (2): 213–62. https://doi.org/10.2475/02.2012.05.

Chamovitz, Daniel. 2017. *What A Plant Knows: A Field Guide to the Senses: Updated and Expanded Edition.* New York: Scientific American/Farrar, Straus and Giroux.

Chen, Jie, Hans Peter Blume, and Lothar Beyer. 2000. "Weathering of Rocks Induced by Lichen Colonization—A Review." *Catena* 39 (2): 121–46. https://doi.org/10.1016/S0341-8162(99)00085-5.

Chitchlow, Keith. 1976. *Islamic Patterns: An Analytical and Cosmological Approach.* New York: Schocken Books.

——. 2011. *The Hidden Geometry of Flowers: Living Rhythms, Form, and Number.* Edinburgh: Floris Books.

Clark, Douglas H., and Alan R. Gillespie. 1997. "Timing and Significance of Late-Glacial and Holocene Cirque Glaciation in the Sierra Nevada, California." *Quaternary International* 38–39 (January): 21–38. https://doi.org/10.1016/s1040-6182(96)00024-9.

Cook, Theodore Andre. 1914. *The Curves of Life.* London: Constable and Company.

Cooper, Sheldon J., and James A. Gessaman. 2005. "Nocturnal Hypothermia in Seasonally Acclimatized Mountain Chickadees and Juniper Titmice." *Condor* 107 (1): 151–55. https://doi.org/10.1650/7597.

Crawford, Stuart D. 2019. "Lichens Used in Traditional Medicine." In *Lichen Secondary Metabolites,* ed. Branislav Ranković, 31–97. Cham: Springer International Publishing. https://doi.org/10.1007/978-3-030-16814-8_2.

Cushing, Frank Hamilton. 1991. *Zuni Fetishes.* Las Vegas: KC Publications.

DeByle N. V., and R. P Winokur, eds. 1985. *Aspen: Ecology and Management in the Western United States. U.S. Department of Agriculture Forest Service General Technical Report RM-119.* Fort Collinis, CO.

DeCelles, P. G. 2004. "Late Jurassic to Eocene Evolution of the Cordilleran Thrust Belt and Foreland Basin System, Western U.S.A." *American Journal of Science* 304 (2): 105–68. https://doi.org/10.2475/ajs.304.2.105.

Despain, Joel. 2003. *Hidden Beneath the Mountains: The Caves of Sequoia and Kings Canyon National Parks.* Dayton: Cave Books.

Dickinson, Emily. 1951. *The Complete Poems of Emily Dickinson.* Edited by Thomas H. Johnson. New York: Little Brown and Company.

——. 1958. *Selected Letters.* Edited by Thomas H. Johnson. Cambridge: Belknap Press of Harvard University Press.

Drake, Aaron, Tammy L. Haut Donahue, Mitchel Stansloski, Karen Fox, Benjamin B. Wheatley, and Seth W. Donahue. 2016. "Horn and Horn Core Trabecular Bone of Bighorn Sheep Rams Absorbs Impact Energy and Reduces Brain Cavity Accelerations during High Impact Ramming of the Skull." *Acta Biomaterialia* 44 (October): 41–50. https://doi.org/10.1016/j.actbio.2016.08.019.

Egan, Timoth. 2010. *The Big Burn: Teddy Roosevelt and the Fire That Saved America*. New York: Houghton Mifflin Harcourt.

Epanchin, Peter N., Roland A. Knapp, and Sharon P. Lawler. 2010. "Nonnative Trout Impact an Alpine-Nesting Bird by Altering Aquatic-Insect Subsidies." *Ecology* 91 (8): 2406–15. https://doi.org/10.1890/09-1974.1.

Fenn, Mark E., Jill S. Baron, Edith B. Allen, Heather M. Rueth, Koren R. Nydick, Linda Geiser, William D. Bowman, et al. 2003. "Ecological Effects of Nitrogen Deposition in the Western United States." *BioScience*. American Institute of Biological Sciences. https://doi.org/10.1641/0006-3568(2003)053[0404:EEONDI]2.0.CO;2.

Fettig, Christopher J., Leif A. Mortenson, Beverly M. Bulaon, and Patra B. Foulk. 2019. "Tree Mortality Following Drought in the Central and Southern Sierra Nevada, California, U.S." *Forest Ecology and Management* 432 (January): 164–78. https://doi.org/10.1016/j.foreco.2018.09.006.

Fischer, Karen N., John W. Prather, and Alexander Cruz. 2002. "Nest Site Characteristics and Reproductive Success of the Western Tanager (Piranga Ludoviciana) on the Colorado Front Range." *Western North American Naturalist* 62 (4): 479–83. http://www.jstor.org/stable/41717236.

Forche, Carolyn. 1982. *The Country between Us*. New York: Harper Perennial.

Forshee, Shannon. 2018. "Life on the Edge: Risk of Predation Drives Selection of Habitat and Survival of Neonates in Endangered Sierra Nevada Bighorn Sheep." MS thesis, University of Montana. https://scholarworks.umt.edu/etd/11296.

Franz, Julia. 2016. "Scientists Try to Save This Frog Species from Being Wiped out by Fungus." *World*. 2016. https://www.pri.org/stories/2016-10-08/scientists-try-save-frog-species-being-wiped-out-fungus.

Freas, Cody A., Lara D. LaDage, Timothy C. Roth, and Vladimir V. Pravosudov. 2012. "Elevation-Related Differences in Memory and the Hippocampus in Mountain Chickadees, Poecile Gambeli." *Animal Behaviour* 84 (1): 121–27. https://doi.org/10.1016/j.anbehav.2012.04.018.

Gillespie, Alan R., and Paul H. Zehfuss. 2004. "Glaciations of the Sierra Nevada, California, USA." *Developments in Quaternary Science* 2 (PART B): 51–62. https://doi.org/10.1016/S1571-0866(04)80185-4.

Gillespie, Alison. 2006. "Environmental Records in a High-Altitude Low-Latitude Glacier, Sierra Nevada, California." MS thesis, Western Washington University. https://cedar.wwu.edu/wwuet/794.

Glazner, Allen F., and Greg M. Stock. 2010. *Geology Underfoot in Yosemite National Park*. Missoula: Mountain Press Publishing Company.

Goulden, M. L., and R. C. Bales. 2019. "California Forest Die-off Linked to Multi-Year Deep Soil Drying in 2012–2015 Drought." *Nature Geoscience* 12 (8): 632–37. https://doi.org/10.1038/s41561-019-0388-5.

Graham, Daniel W. 2019. "Heraclitus." In *The Stanford Encyclopedia of Philosophy*, Stanford University, 1997–. Article published February 8, 2007, revised September 3, 2019. https://plato.stanford.edu/entries/heraclitus/.

Graumlich, Lisa J. 1993. "A 1000-Year Record of Temperature and Precipitation in the Sierra Nevada." *Quaternary Research* 39 (2): 249–55. https://doi.org/10.1006/qres.1993.1029.

Green, Bill. 2008. *Water, Ice & Stone: Science and Memory on the Antarctic Lakes*. New York: Belleview Literary Press.

Grinnell, J., and T. I. Storer. 1924. *Animal Life in the Yosemite*. Berkeley: University of California Press. https://www.nps.gov/parkhistory/online_books/grpo/contents.htm.

Grosch, Eugene G., and Robert M. Hazen. 2015. "Microbes, Mineral Evolution, and the Rise of Microcontinents—Origin and Coevolution of Life with Early Earth." *Astrobiology* 15 (10): 922–39. https://doi.org/10.1089/ast.2015.1302.

Grotzinger, John, and Thomas H. Jordan. 2019. *Understanding Earth*. Eighth. New York: W.H. Freeman.

Gruell, Charles E. 2001. *Fire in Sierra Nevada Forests: A Photographic Interpretation of Ecological Change Since 1849*. Missoula: Mountain Press.

Haas, Robert, ed. 1995. *The Essential Haiku: Versions of Basho, Buson, and Issa*. New York: Ecco Press.

Hanken, James, and Paul W. Sherman. 1981. "Multiple Paternity in Belding's Ground Squirrel Litters." *Science* 212 (4492): 351–53. https://doi.org/10.1126/science.7209536.

Hanson, Chad T. 2013. "Habitat Use of Pacific Fishers in a Heterogeneous Post-Fire and Unburned Forest Landscape on the Kern Plateau, Sierra Nevada, California." *Open Forest Science Journal* 6: 24–30. https://doi.org/10.2174/1874398601306010024.

Hanson, Chad T., and Dennis C. Odion. 2016. "Historical Forest Conditions within the Range of the Pacific Fisher and Spotted Owl in the Central and Southern Sierra Nevada, California, USA." *Natural Areas Journal* 36 (1): 8–19. https://doi.org/10.3375/043.036.0106.

Harris, Roger D. 1980. "Decay Characteristics of Pilleated Woodpecker Nest Trees." In *Snag Habitat Management Symposium, Northern Arizona University, Flagstaff*. Flagstaff, AZ: Northern Arizona University.

Hartesveldt, R. J., and H. T. Harvey. 1967. "The Fire Ecology of Sequoia Regeneration." In *Proceedings of the 7th Tall Timbers Fire Ecology Conference, Tall Timbers Research Station, Tallahassee, FL*, 65–77. Tallahassee, FL: Tall Timbers Research Station and Land Conservancy.

Heinrich, Bernd. 2015. *The Homing Instinct: Meaning and Mystery in Animal Migration*. Boston: Mariner Books Houghton Mifflin Harcourt.

Henry, Christopher D., Nicholas H. Hinz, James E. Faulds, Joseph P. Colgan, David A. John, Elwood R. Brooks, Elizabeth J. Cassel, Larry J. Garside, David A. Davis, and Steven B. Castor. 2012. "Eocene-Early Miocene Paleotopography of the Sierra Nevada-Great Basin-Nevadaplano Based on Widespread Ash-Flow Tuffs and Paleovalleys." *Geosphere* 8 (1): 1–27. https://doi.org/10.1130/GES00727.1.

Hill, Mary. 2006. *Geology of the Sierra Nevada*. Revised ed. Berkeley: University of California Press.

Hodgson, Susan Fox. 2007. "Obsidian: Sacred Glass from the California Sky." *Geological Society Special Publication* 273 (1): 295–313. https://doi.org/10.1144/GSL.SP.2007.273.01.23.

Hogg, John T. 1984. "Mating in Bighorn Sheep: Multiple Creative Male Strategies." *Science* 225 (4661): 526–29. https://doi.org/10.1126/science.6539948.

Hudon, Jocelyn. 1991. "Unusual Carotenoid Use by the Western Tanager (Piranga Ludoviciana) and Its Evolutionary Implications." *Canadian Journal of Zoology* 69 (9): 2311–20. https://doi.org/10.1139/z91-325.

———. 2020. *Western Tanager Piranga Ludoviciana, Version 1.0*. Edited by A. F. Poole and F. B. Gill. *Birds of the World*. Ithaca, NY: Cornell Lab of Ornithology.

Humphreys, Eugene, Erin Hessler, Kenneth Dueker, G. Lang Farmer, Eric Erslev, and Tanya Atwater. 2003. "How Laramide-Age Hydration of North American Lithosphere by the Farallon Slab Controlled Subsequent Activity in the Western United States." *International Geology Review* 45 (7): 575–95. https://doi.org/10.2747/0020-6814.45.7.575.

Illah, Ibn 'Ata.' 1978. *The Book of Wisdom*. Translated by Victor Danner. New York: Pauist Press.

Issa, Kobayashi. 1979. *The Spring of My Life and Selected Haiku*. Translated by Sam Hamill. Boulder: Shambhala Publications.

James, David G., and David Nunnallee. 2011. *Life Histories of Cascadia Butterflies*. Corvallis: Oregon State University Press.

Jennings, W. Bryan, David F. Bradford, and Dale F. Johnson. 1992. "Dependence of the Garter Snake Thamnophis Elegans on Amphibians in the Sierra Nevada of California." *Journal of Herpetology* 26 (4): 503–5. https://doi.org/10.2307/1565132.

Johnson, Heather. 2010. "Escaping the Extinction Vortex: Identifying Factors Affecting Population Performance and Recovery in Endangered Sierra Nevada Bighorn Sheep." PhD diss., University of Montana. https://scholarworks.umt.edu/etd/379.

Jones, Gavin M, R. J Gutiérrez, Douglas J. Tempel, Sheila A. Whitmore, William J. Berigan, and M. Zachariah Peery. 2016. "Megafires: An Emerging Threat to Old-Forest Species." *Frontiers in Ecology and the Environment* 14 (6): 300–306. https://doi.org/10.1002/fee.1298.

Jovan, Sarah, and Tom Carlberg. 2007. "Nitrogen Content of Letharia Vulpina Tissue from Forests of the Sierra Nevada, California: Geographic Patterns and Relationships to Ammonia Estimates and Climate." *Environmental Monitoring and Assessment* 129 (1–3): 243–51. https://doi.org/10.1007/s10661-006-9357-8.

Jovan, Sarah, and Bruce McCune. 2006. "Using Epiphytic Macrolichen Communities for Biomonitoring Ammonia in Forests of the Greater Sierra Nevada, California." *Water, Air, and Soil Pollution* 170 (1–4): 69–93. https://doi.org/10.1007/s11270-006-2814-8.

Kelly, Anne E., and Michael L. Goulden. 2016. "A Montane Mediterranean Climate Supports Year-Round Photosynthesis and High Forest Biomass." *Tree Physiology* 36 (4): 459–68. https://doi.org/10.1093/treephys/tpv131.

Kelsey, Rodd. 2019. *Wildfires and Forest Resilience: The Case for Ecological Forestry in the Sierra Nevada. Unpublished Report of The Nature Conservancy*. Sacramento, CA. https://www.scienceforconservation.org/products/wildfires-and-forest-resilience.

Keskitalo, Johanna, Gustaf Bergquist, Per Gardeström, and Stefan Jansson. 2005. "A Cellular Timetable of Autumn Senescence." *Plant Physiology* 139 (4): 1635–48. https://doi.org/10.1104/pp.105.066845.

Kılıç, Nil, Sümer Aras, and Demet Cansaran-Duman. 2018. "Determination of Vulpinic Acid Effect on Apoptosis and mRNA Expression Levels in Breast Cancer Cell Lines." *Anti-Cancer Agents in Medicinal Chemistry* 18 (14): 2032–41. https://doi.org/10.2174/1871520618666180903101803.

King, Heather. 2007. "The Closest to Love We'll Ever Get." *Portland Magazine*, 2007.

King, Martin Luther. 1965. "Speech by Martin Luther King given at Syracuse University on July 15, 1965." Syracuse, New York.

Knapp, Roland A. 1996. "Non-Native Trout in Natural Lakes of the Sierra Nevada: An Analysis of Their Distribution and Impacts on Native Aquatic Biota, in Sierra Nevada

Ecosystem Project (SNEP)-Final Report to Congress (Vol. II), Chapter 8: Assessments and Scientific Basis for M." In *Sierra Nevada Ecosystem Project: Final Report to Congress, Vol. III, Assessments and Scientific Basis for Management Options*, edited by Don C. Erman, 363–407. Davis, CA: University of California Davis, Centers for Water and Wildland Resources. https://mountainlakesresearch.com/wp-content/uploads/2018/12/Knapp_SNEP_VIII_C08.pdf.

———. 2005. "Effects of Nonnative Fish and Habitat Characteristics on Lentic Herpetofauna in Yosemite National Park, USA." *Biological Conservation* 121 (2): 265–79. https://doi.org/10.1016/j.biocon.2004.05.003.

Knapp, Roland A., Daniel M. Boiano, and Vance T. Vredenburg. 2007. "Removal of Nonnative Fish Results in Population Expansion of a Declining Amphibian (Mountain Yellow-Legged Frog, Rana Muscosa)." *Biological Conservation* 135 (1): 11–20. https://doi.org/10.1016/J.BIOCON.2006.09.013.

Knapp, Roland A., Gary M. Fellers, Patrick M. Kleeman, David A. W. Miller, Vance T. Vredenburg, Erica Bree Rosenblum, and Cheryl J. Briggs. 2016. "Large-Scale Recovery of an Endangered Amphibian despite Ongoing Exposure to Multiple Stressors." *Proceedings of the National Academy of Sciences of the United States of America* 113 (42): 11889–94. https://doi.org/10.1073/pnas.1600983113.

Kozlovsky, Dovid Y., Carrie L. Branch, and Vladimir V. Pravosudov. 2015. "Problem-Solving Ability and Response to Novelty in Mountain Chickadees (Poecile Gambeli) from Different Elevations." *Behavioral Ecology and Sociobiology* 69 (4): 635–43. https://doi.org/10.1007/s00265-015-1874-4.

Lanner, Ronald M. 1996. *Made for Each Other: A Symbiosis of Birds and Pines*. New York: Oxford University Press.

Laws, John Muir. 2007. *Laws Field Guide To The Sierra Nevada*. Berkeley: Heydey Books.

Libbrecht, Kenneth G. 2005. "The Physics of Snow Crystals." *Reports on Progress in Physics* 66 (4): 855. https://doi.org/doi:10.1088/0034-4885/68/4/R03.

Libbrecht, Kenneth, and Patricia Rasmussen. 2003. *The Snowflake: Winter's Secret Beauty*. Stillwater: Voyageur Press.

Liu, Lijun, Michael Gurnis, Maria Seton, Jason Saleeby, R. Dietmar Müller, and Jennifer M. Jackson. 2010. "The Role of Oceanic Plateau Subduction in the Laramide Orogeny." *Nature Geoscience* 3 (5): 353–57. https://doi.org/10.1038/ngeo829.

Liu, Xiaobo, Robert J. Koestler, Thomas Warscheid, Yoko Katayama, and Ji Dong Gu. 2020. "Microbial Deterioration and Sustainable Conservation of Stone Monuments and Buildings." *Nature Sustainability*. Nature Research. https://doi.org/10.1038/s41893-020-00602-5.

Lockwood, John P., and James G. Moore. 1979. "Regional Deformation of the Sierra Nevada, California, on Conjugate Microfault Sets." *Journal of Geophysical Research* 84 (B11): 6041–49. https://doi.org/10.1029/JB084iB11p06041.

Lute, A. C., J. T. Abatzoglou, and K. C. Hegewisch. 2015. "Projected Changes in Snowfall Extremes and Interannual Variability of Snowfall in the Western United States." *Water Resources Research* 51 (2): 960–72. https://doi.org/10.1002/2014WR016267.

MacGinitie, Harry D. 1941. *A Middle Eocene Flora from the Central Sierra Nevada, Carnegie Institution of Washington Publication 534*. Washington, D.C.: Carnegie Institution of Washington. http://hdl.handle.net/2027/uc1.31822012272068.

Marks, Karen A, Daniel L Vizconde, Emma S Gibson, Jennifer R Rodriguez, and Scott Nunes. 2017. "Play Behavior and Responses to Novel Situations in Juvenile Ground Squirrels." *Journal of Mammalogy* 98 (4): 1202–10. https://doi.org/10.1093/jmammal/gyx049.

Marmelzat, Willard L. 1987. "History of Dermatologic Surgery from the Beginnings to Late Antiquity." *Clinics in Dermatology* 5 (4): 1–10. https://doi.org/10.1016/0738-081X(87)90023-X.

Martel, Stephen J. 2017. "Progress in Understanding Sheeting Joints over the Past Two Centuries." *Journal of Structural Geology*. Elsevier Ltd. https://doi.org/10.1016/j.jsg.2016.11.003.

Mast, M. Alisa, David A. Alvarez, and Steven D. Zaugg. 2012. "Deposition and Accumulation of Airborne Organic Contaminants in Yosemite National Park, California." *Environmental Toxicology and Chemistry* 31 (3): 524–33. https://doi.org/10.1002/etc.1727.

Mateo, Jill M. 2003. "Kin Recognition in Ground Squirrels and Other Rodents." *Journal of Mammalogy* 84 (4): 1163–81. https://doi.org/10.1644/BLe-011.

——. 2017. "The Ontogeny of Kin-Recognition Mechanisms in Belding's Ground Squirrels." *Physiology and Behavior* 173 (May): 279–84. https://doi.org/10.1016/j.physbeh.2017.02.024.

——. 2020. "Belding's Ground Squirrels." *Mono Basin Clearinghouse*. https://www.monobasinresearch.org/research/squirrels.php.

Matsushita, Atsuko, Hiroko Awata, Motohiro Wakakuwa, Shin-ya Takemura, and Kentaro Arikawa. 2012. "Rhabdom Evolution in Butterflies: Insights from the Uniquely Tiered and Heterogeneous Ommatidia of the Glacial Apollo Butterfly, *Parnassius Glacialis*." *Proceedings of the Royal Society B: Biological Sciences* 279 (1742): 3482–90. https://doi.org/10.1098/rspb.2012.0475.

Matthews, Robert W., and Janice R. Matthews. 2010. "Defense: A Survival Catalogue." In *Insect Behavior*, 185–215. Dordrecht: Springer. https://doi.org/10.1007/978-90-481-2389-6_5.

McCormac, Jim, and Ray E. Showman. 2009. "Lichen Composition in Blue-Gray Gnatcatcher and Ruby-Throated Hummingbird Nests." *Ohio Cardinal*, Fall 2009: 72–82.

McCowan, Brenda, and Stacie L. Hooper. 2002. "Individual Acoustic Variation in Belding's Ground Squirrel Alarm Chirps in the High Sierra Nevada." *Journal of the Acoustical Society of America* 111 (3): 1157–60. https://doi.org/10.1121/1.1446048.

McCune, B., J. Grenon, L.S. Mutch, and E.P. Martin. 2007. "Lichens in Relation to Management Issues in the Sierra Nevada National Parks." *Pacific Northwest Fungi* 2 (3): 1–39. https://doi.org/10.2509/pnwf.2007.002.003.

McKelvey, Kevin S., Carl N. Skinner, Chi-ru Chang, Don C. Etman, Susan J. Husari, David J. Parsons, Jan van Wagtendonk, and Phillip C Weatherspoon. 1996. "An Overview of Fire in the Sierra Nevada," in *Sierra Nevada Ecosystem Project: Final Report to Congress, Vol. II, Assessments and Scientific Basis for Management Options*, 1033–40. Davis, CA: University of California Davis, Centers for Water and Wildland Resources. https://www.fs.fed.us/psw/publications/mckelvey/mckelvey2.PDF.

McPhillips, Devin, and Mark T. Brandon. 2012. "Topographic Evolution of the Sierra Nevada Measured Directly by Inversion of Low Temperature Thermochronology." *American Journal of Science* 312 (2): 90–116. http://dx.doi.org/10.2475/02.2012.02

Meldahl, Keith Heyer. 2011. *Rough-Hewn Land: A Geologic Journey from California to the Rocky Mountains*. Berkeley: University of California Press.

Merwin, W. S. 1973. *Asian Figures*. New York: Atheneum.

Millar, Constance I., and Wallace B. Woolfenden. 1999. "Sierra Nevada Forests: Where Did They Come from? Where Are They Going? What Does It Mean?" In *Natural Resource Management: Perceptions and Realties. Transactions of the the 64th North American Wildlife and Natural Resources Conference*, edited by R. McCabe, 206–36. San Francisco. Washington, D.C.: Wildlife Management Institute.

Mitton, Jeffry B., and Michael C. Grant. 1996. "Genetic Variation and the Natural History of Quaking Aspen." *BioScience* 46 (1): 25–31. https://doi.org/10.2307/1312652.

Moore, James G., and Barry C. Moring. 2013. "Rangewide Glaciation in the Sierra Nevada, California." *Geosphere* 9 (6): 1804–18. https://doi.org/10.1130/GES00891.1.

Moore, James Gregory. 2000. *Exploring the Highest Sierra*. Stanford: Stanford University Press.

Moritz, Craig, James L. Patton, Chris J. Conroy, Juan L. Parra, Gary C. White, and Steven R. Beissinger. 2008. "Impact of a Century of Climate Change on Small-Mammal Communities in Yosemite National Park, USA." *Science* 322 (5899): 261–64. https://doi.org/10.1126/science.1163428.

Morton, Martin L., and Paul W. Sherman. 1978. "Effects of a Spring Snowstorm on Behavior, Reproduction, and Survival of Belding's Ground Squirrels." *Canadian Journal of Zoology* 56 (12): 2578–90. https://doi.org/10.1139/z78-346.

Muir, John. 1912. *The Yosemite*. New York: The Century Company.

Myer, Gregory D., David Smith, Kim D. Barber Foss, Christopher A. Dicesare, Adam W. Kiefer, Adam M. Kushner, Staci M. Thomas, Heidi Sucharew, and Jane C. Khoury. 2014. "Rates of Concussion Are Lower in National Football League Games Played at Higher Altitudes." *Journal of Orthopaedic & Sports Physical Therapy* 44 (3): 164–72. https://doi.org/10.2519/jospt.2014.5298.

National Park Service. 2015. *Bighorn Sheep, Yosemite Nature Notes Episode 27*. Video, 8 minutes 58 seconds. Yosemite Conservancy. https://www.nps.gov/media/video/view.htm?id=9C88ABB3-1DD8-B71B-0BA0B67F3AB4BBBE.

Neruda, Pablo. 2001. *The Book of Questions*. Translated by William O'Daly. Port Townsend: Copper Canyon Press.

Nishida, R., and M. Rothschild. 1995. "A Cyanoglucoside Stored by a Sedum-Feeding Apollo Butterfly, Parnassius Phoebus." *Experientia* 51 (3): 267–69. https://doi.org/10.1007/BF01931110.

Oliver, Mary. 2017. *Devotions: The Selected Poems of Mary Oliver*. New York: Penguin.

Paterson, Scott R., and Othmar T. Tobisch. 1992. "Rates of Processes in Magmatic Arcs: Implications for the Timing and Nature of Pluton Emplacement and Wall Rock Deformation." *Journal of Structural Geology* 14 (3): 291–300. https://doi.org/10.1016/0191-8141(92)90087-D.

Pearson, L. C., and D. B. Lawrence. 1958. "Photosynthesis in Aspen Bark." *American Journal of Botany* 45 (5): 383. https://doi.org/10.2307/2439638.

Phinney, Nathan H., Yngvar Gauslaa, and Knut Asbjørn Solhaug. 2019. "Why Chartreuse? The Pigment Vulpinic Acid Screens Blue Light in the Lichen Letharia Vulpina." *Planta* 249 (3): 709–18. https://doi.org/10.1007/s00425-018-3034-3.

Phoenix, G. K., and M. C. Press. 2005. "Linking Physiological Traits to Impacts on Community Structure and Function: The Role of Root Hemiparasitic Orobanchaceae (Ex-Scrophulariaceae)." *Journal of Ecology* 93: 67–78. http://www.jstor.org/stable/3599458.

Press, Malcolm C. 2016. "Dracula or Robin Hood ? A Functional Role for Root Hemiparasites in Nutrient Poor Ecosystems." *Oikos* 82 (3): 609–11. http://www.jstor.org/stable/3546383.

Prum, Richard O. 2018. *The Evolution of Beauty: How Darwin's Forgotten Theory of Mate Choice Shapes the Animal World—and Us*. New York: Anchor Books.

Pruppacher, H., and J. Klett. 2010. *Microstructure of Atmospheric Clouds and Precipitation. Atmospheric and Oceanographic Sciences Library, Vol 18.* Dordrecht: Springer.

Rauscher, Sara A., Jeremy S. Pal, Noah S. Diffenbaugh, and Michael M. Benedetti. 2008. "Future Changes in Snowmelt-Driven Runoff Timing over the Western US." *Geophysical Research Letters* 35 (16). https://doi.org/10.1029/2008GL034424.

Reed, Johannah. 2012. "Hemiparasitic Castilleja Promotes Plant Diversity in an Alpine Meadow Ecosystem." BS thesis, University of Tennessee. https://trace.tennessee.edu/utk_chanhonoproj/1550.

Robinson, Scott R. 1981. "Alarm Communication in Belding's Ground Squirrels." *Zeitschrift für Tierpsychologie* 56 (2): 150–68. https://doi.org/10.1111/j.1439-0310.1981.tb01293.x.

Rosen, Julia. 2017. "The Cost of the Bighorn Comeback." *High Country News*, May 29, 2017.

Rosing, Minik T., Dennis K. Bird, Norman H. Sleep, William Glassley, and Francis Albarede. 2006. "The Rise of Continents—An Essay on the Geologic Consequences of Photosynthesis." *Palaeogeography, Palaeoclimatology, Palaeoecology* 232 (2–4): 99–113. https://doi.org/10.1016/j.palaeo.2006.01.007.

Rother, M., A. Sala, Z. Holden, K. Davis, P. Higuera, S. Parks, T. Veblen, M. Maneta, and S. Dobrowski. 2019. "Wildfires and Climate Change Push Low-Elevation Forests across a Critical Climate Threshold for Tree Regeneration." *Proceedings of the National Academy of Sciences of the United States of America* 116 (13). https://doi.org/10.1073/pnas.1815107116.

Ruddiman, William F. 2013. *Earth's Climate: Past, Present, and Future.* 3rd ed. New York: W.H. Freeman.

Rumi, Jalaludin. 1979. *Teaching of Rumi: The Masnavi. Abridged and Translated by E.H. Whinfield.* London: Octagon Press.

Safford, H. D., and Jens T. Stevens. 2017. *Natural Range of Variation (NRV) for Yellow Pine and Mixed Conifer Forests in the Sierra Nevada, Southern Cascades, and Modoc and Inyo National Forests, California, USA, General Technical Report.* PSW-GTR-256. Albany, CA.

Samuel, Cheryl. 1982. *The Chilkat Dancing Blanket.* Seattle: Pacific Search Press.

Sanai, Hakim. 1974. *The Walled Garden of Truth.* Translated and abridged by David Pendlebury. London: Octagon Press.

Saunders, Clive. 2008. "Charge Separation Mechanisms in Clouds." *Space Science Reviews* 137: 335–53. https://doi.org/10.1007/978-0-387-87664-1_22.

Scheele, Ben C., Frank Pasmans, Lee F. Skerratt, Lee Berger, An Martel, Wouter Beukema, Aldemar A. Acevedo, et al. 2019. "Amphibian Fungal Panzootic Causes Catastrophic and Ongoing Loss of Biodiversity." *Science* 363 (6434): 1459–63. https://doi.org/10.1126/science.aav0379.

Schindler, Daniel E., Roland A. Knapp, and Peter R. Leavitt. 2001. "Alteration of Nutrient Cycles and Algal Production Resulting from Fish Introductions into Mountain Lakes." *Ecosystems* 4 (4): 308–21. https://doi.org/10.1007/s10021-001-0013-4.

Schwartz, Mark W., Nathalie Butt, Christopher R. Dolanc, Andrew Holguin, Max A. Moritz, Malcolm P. North, Hugh D. Safford, Nathan L. Stephenson, James H. Thorne, and Phillip J. van Mantgem. 2015. "Increasing Elevation of Fire in the Sierra Nevada and Implications for Forest Change." *Ecosphere* 6 (7): 1–10. https://doi.org/10.1890/ES15-00003.1.

Scott, James A. 1974. "Population Biology and Adult Behavior of the Circumpolar Butterfly, Parnassius Phoebus F. (Papilionidae)." *Insect Systematics & Evolution* 4 (3): iii–168. https://doi.org/10.1163/187631274X00010.

Shabistari, Mahmud. 2007. *The Garden of Mystery*. Translated by Robert Abdul Hayy Carr. Cambridge: Archetype.

Shah, Idries. 1989. *The Dermis Probe*. London: Octagon Press.

——. 2015. *Caravan of Dreams*. London: ISF Publishing.

——. 2017. *The Way of the Sufi*. London: ISF Publishing.

Shapiro, Arthur M. 1996. "Status of Butterflies," in *Sierra Nevada Ecosystem Project: Final Report to Congress, Vol. II, Assessments and Scientific Basis for Management Options*, 743–57. Davis, CA: University of California Davis, Centers for Water and Wildland Resources. https://pubs.usgs.gov/dds/dds-43/VOL_II/VII_C27.PDF.

Sharp, Robert P., and Allen F. Glazner. 1997. *Geology Underfoot in Death Valley and Owens Valley*. Missoula: Mountain Press Publishing Company.

Sherman, Paul W. 1977. "Nepotism and the Evolution of Alarm Calls." *Science* 197 (4310): 1246–53. https://doi.org/10.1126/science.197.4310.1246.

——. 1980. "The Meaning of Nepotism." *The American Naturalist* 116 (4): 604-606. https://doi.org/10.1086/283652.

——. 1981. "Kinship, Demography, and Belding's Ground Squirrel Nepotism." *Behavioral Ecology and Sociobiology* 8 (4): 251–59. https://doi.org/10.1007/BF00299523.

——. 1985. "Alarm Calls of Belding's Ground Squirrels to Aerial Predators: Nepotism or Self-Preservation?" *Behavioral Ecology and Sociobiology*. https://doi.org/10.1007/BF00293209.

Shields, William M. 1980. "Ground Squirrel Alarm Calls: Nepotism or Parental Care?" *The American Naturalist* 116 (4): 599-603. https://doi.org/10.1086/283651.

Shrestha, Gajendra, Andrew Thompson, Richard Robison, and Larry L. St. Clair. 2016. "Letharia Vulpina, a Vulpinic Acid Containing Lichen, Targets Cell Membrane and Cell Division Processes in Methicillin-Resistant Staphylococcus Aureus." *Pharmaceutical Biology* 54 (3): 413–18. https://doi.org/10.3109/13880209.2015.1038754.

Shunk, Stephen A. 2016. *Peterson Reference Guide to Woodpeckers of North America*. Boston: Houghton Mifflin Harcourt.

Slansky, Frank. 1979. "Effect of the Lichen Chemicals Atranorin and Vulpinic Acid upon Feeding and Growth of Larvae of the Yellow-Striped Armyworm, Spodoptera Ornithogalli." *Environmental Entomology* 8 (5): 865–68. https://doi.org/10.1093/ee/8.5.865.

Spawn, S. A., and H. K. Gibbs. 2010. *Global Aboveground and Belowground Biomass Carbon Density Maps for the Year 2010*. Oak Ridge: ORNL DAAC. https://doi.org/10.3334/ORNLDAAC/1763.

Spribille, Toby, Veera Tuovinen, Philipp Resl, Dan Vanderpool, Heimo Wolinski, M. Catherine Aime, Kevin Schneider, et al. 2016. "Basidiomycete Yeasts in the Cortex of Ascomycete Macrolichens." *Science* 353 (6298): 488–92. https://doi.org/10.1126/science.aaf8287.

Stebbins, R. C. 2003. *A Field Guide to Western Reptiles and Amphibians*. Third edit. Boston: Houghton Mifflin Company.

Stephens, Scott L., A. LeRoy Westerling, Matthew D. Hurteau, M. Zachariah Peery, Courtney A. Schultz, and Sally Thompson. 2020. "Fire and Climate Change: Conserving Seasonally Dry

Forests Is Still Possible." *Frontiers in Ecology and the Environment* 18 (6): 354–60. https://doi. org/10.1002/fee.2218.

Stephenson, Nathan L. 2000. "Estimated Ages of Some Large Giant Sequoias: General Sherman Keeps Getting Younger." *Madroño* 47 (1): 61–67. https://www.jstor.org/stable/41425345.

Stephenson, Nathan L., and Philip W. Rundel. 1979. "Quantitative Variation and the Ecological Role of Vulpinic Acid and Atranorin in Thallus of Letharia Vulpina." *Biochemical Systematics and Ecology* 7 (4): 263–67. https://doi.org/10.1016/0305-1978(79)90003-6.

Stevens, Peter. 1974. *Patterns in Nature*. Boston: Little Brown and Company.

Stewart, Ian. 2011. *The Mathematics of Life*. New York: Basic Books.

Svanberg, Ingvar, and Sabira Ståhlberg. 2017. "Killing Wolves with Lichens: Wolf Lichen, Letharia Vulpina (L.) Hue, in Scandinavian Folk Biology." *Swedish Dialects and Folk Traditions* 140: 173–87.

Sydor, Maciej, Grzegorz Pinkowski, and Anna Jasí. 2020. "The Brinell Method for Determining Hardness of Wood Flooring Materials." *Forests* 11: 878. https://doi.org/10.3390/f11080878.

Szyrmer, Wanda, and Isztar Zawadzki. 2010. "Snow Studies. Part II: Average Relationship between Mass of Snowflakes and Their Terminal Fall Velocity." *Journal of the Atmospheric Sciences* 67 (10): 3319–35. https://doi.org/10.1175/2010JAS3390.1.

Thoreau, Henry David. 2006. *Walden*. New Haven: Yale University Press.

Tingley, Morgan W., Andrew N. Stillman, Robert L. Wilkerson, Sarah C. Sawyer, and Rodney B. Siegel. 2020. "Black-Backed Woodpecker Occupancy in Burned and Beetle-Killed Forests: Disturbance Agent Matters." *Forest Ecology and Management* 455 (January): 117694. https://doi.org/10.1016/j.foreco.2019.117694.

Turnbaugh, S. P., and W. A. Turnbaugh. 1986. *Indian Baskets*. West Chester, PA: Schiffer Publishing Ltd.

U.S. Fish and Wildlife Service. 2007. *Recovery Plan for the Sierra Nevada Bighorn Sheep*. Sacramento, CA.

Uman, Martin A. 1964. "The Peak Temperature of Lightning." *Journal of Atmospheric and Terrestrial Physics* 26 (1): 123–28. https://doi.org/10.1016/0021-9169(64)90113-8.

Vredenburg, V. T., R. Bingham, R. Knapp, J. A. T. Morgan, C. Moritz, and D. Wake. 2007. "Concordant Molecular and Phenotypic Data Delineate New Taxonomy and Conservation Priorities for the Endangered Mountain Yellow-Legged Frog." *Journal of Zoology* 271 (4): 361–74. https://doi.org/10.1111/j.1469-7998.2006.00258.x.

Wagtendonk, J. W. van, Neil G. Sugihara, Scott L. Stephens, Andrea E. Thode, Kevin E. Shaffer, Jo Ann Fites-Kaufman, and James K. Agee. 2018. *Fire in California's Ecosystems*. Second ed. Berkeley: University of California Press.

Wake, David B, and Vance T Vredenburg. 2008. "Colloquium Paper: Are We in the Midst of the Sixth Mass Extinction? A View from the World of Amphibians." *Proceedings of the National Academy of Sciences of the United States of America* 105 Suppl (August): 11466–73. https://doi.org/10.1073/pnas.0801921105.

Walker, Thayer. 2016. "Giants in the Face of Drought." *Atlantic*, November 2016. https://www.theatlantic.com/science/archive/2016/11/giants-in-the-face-of-drought/508601/.

Wark, McKenzie. 2014. "There Is Another World, and It Is This One." Public Seminar. 2014. https://publicseminar.org/2014/01/there-is-another-world-and-it-is-this-one/.

Wenk, Elizabeth. 2015. *Wildflowers of the High Sierra and John Muir Trail*. Birmingham: Wilderness Press.

Whitaker, J. O. 1980. *The Audubon Society Field Guide to North American Mammals*. New York: A. Knopf.

White, Angela M., Gina L. Tarbill, Robert L. Wilkerson, and Rodney B. Siegel. 2019. "Few Detections of Black-Backed Woodpeckers (Picoides Arcticus) in Extreme Wildfires in the Sierra Nevada." *Avian Conservation and Ecology* 14 (1): 17. https://doi.org/10.5751/ACE-01375-140117.

Wiese, Karen. 2001. *Sierra Nevada Wildflowers*. Helena: Falcon Publishing.

Williams, E. R. 1988. "The Electrification of Thunderstorms." *Scientific American* (November): 88–89.

Williams, Terry Tempest. 1994. *An Unspoken Hunger: Stories from the Field*. New York: Pantheon Books.

Wood, Connor M., and Gavin M. Jones. 2019. "Framing Management of Social-Ecological Systems in Terms of the Cost of Failure: The Sierra Nevada, USA as a Case Study." *Environmental Research Letters* 14 (10): 105004. https://doi.org/10.1088/1748-9326/ab4033.

Woodhams, Douglas C., Vance T. Vredenburg, Mary-Alice Simon, Dean Billheimer, Bashar Shakhtour, Yu Shyr, Cheryl J. Briggs, Louise A. Rollins-Smith, and Reid N. Harris. 2007. "Symbiotic Bacteria Contribute to Innate Immune Defenses of the Threatened Mountain Yellow-Legged Frog, Rana Muscosa." *Biological Conservation* 138 (3–4): 390–98. https://doi.org/10.1016/J.BIOCON.2007.05.004.

Wright, David H., Anh V. Nguyen, and Stacy Anderson. 2016. "Upward Shifts in Recruitment of High-Elevation Tree Species in the Northern Sierra Nevada, California." *California Fish and Game* 102 (1): 17–31.

WWF. 2020. *Living Planet Report 2020—Bending the Curve of Biodiversity Loss*. Edited by R.E.A. Almond, Grooten M., and T. Petersen. Gland, Switzerland: WWF.

Yi, Sang Ah, Ki Hong Nam, Sil Kim, Hae Min So, Rhim Ryoo, Jeung-Whan Han, Ki Hyun Kim, and Jaecheol Lee. 2019. "Vulpinic Acid Controls Stem Cell Fate toward Osteogenesis and Adipogenesis." *Genes* 11 (1): 18. https://doi.org/10.3390/genes11010018.

Yoshida, Satoko, Songkui Cui, Yasunori Ichihashi, and Ken Shirasu. 2016. "The Haustorium, a Specialized Invasive Organ in Parasitic Plants." *Annual Review of Plant Biology* 67 (1): 643–67. https://doi.org/10.1146/annurev-arplant-043015-111702.

Young, Derek J. N., Chhaya M. Werner, Kevin R. Welch, Truman P. Young, Hugh D. Safford, and Andrew M. Latimer. 2019. "Post-fire Forest Regeneration Shows Limited Climate Tracking and Potential for Drought-induced Type Conversion." *Ecology* 100 (2): e02571. https://doi.org/10.1002/ecy.2571.